CORPORATIONS STRIPPED NAKED I

Exposing The AQ Virus

Ed Rychkun

www.edrychkun.com

TABLE OF CONTENTS

PREFACE   5
1. AQ BASICS EXPLAINED   13
2. THE AQ PROCESS IN ACTION   24
3. MEASURING YOUR AQ   39
4. EFFECT OF AQ'ISM ON PRODUCTIVITY   47
5. THE CORPORATE HIERARCHY   54
6. AQ DISEQUILIBRIUM   65
7. SO HOW'S YOUR AQ TODAY   71
   Case 1: Scooter Blastoff   82
   Case 2: Oscar Ostrich   83
   Case 3: Eric von Shithead   84
   Case 4: Donna Dingdong   85
8. WHY NOT HAVE A MEETING?   87
   The Business of Meetings   87
   Meetings – the Medium of Progress   89
   Steadfast Meat Packers Ltd. – a General Profile   93
   The Meeting Agenda   96
   The Executive Meeting   99
9. LET'S MEET THE DECISION MAKERS   101
   Franklin P. Hardass   102
   Angus P. Steadfast   104
   Scab Dancer   107
   Murk D. Muddler   111
   Flash E. Spreadsheet   114
   Herbert Q. Hoyle   118
   Slink D. Wirlwind   120
   Scooter Blastoff   123
   Now Some of the Victims   126
   Randolf Snooper   127
   Clepto Superbyte   128
10. THE BIG EXECUTIVE MEETING   133

So What's the Big Deal About Meetings?	157
So What's the Secrets?	157
The Corporate Playground - or Battleground?	159

11. A CLOSER LOOK AT EXECUTIVES — 165

The Corporate Executive	163
The Executives - What Makes Them So Great?	167
The Great Transition	172
Boardroom Brawling	174
The Laws of Executive Regression	175
The Six Executive Arsenals	177
The Offensive Arsenal	178
The Defensive Arsenal	184
The Aversive Arsenal	190
The Troublemaker Arsenal	196
The Cultural Arsenal	202
The Manipulator Arsenal	208
So How's Your AQ Today	211

12 THE BOTTOM LINE: A ZERO AQ — 216

The Four Choices	216
The Deep Lesson Here	218
The Law Of Cause And Effect	220

PREFACE

Before you read another sentence, I want you to understand clearly that this book is my own personal satire of the corporate world. It is my view of corporations stripped naked of their glamour and efficiency. When I look back at how I climbed the "ladder of success" to take on positions of CEO, Partner, Director, Owner and Chairman... all those supposedly respected positions, I realize there wasn't really a lot of things learned at University that helped me get there. Perhaps I was lucky but I think perhaps I learned some things that were just not taught in school. What became apparent in the climb was what I saw as the "underbelly" of a corporation and a certain behavior in successful people that went far outside of the normal MBA training. What was so interesting to me was that there was a huge textbook of unwritten material on how people actually succeed to power and position in a corporation without following the traditional management stuff. This book is where I bring this unwritten material to you. It strips companies of their usual look and practices thereby revealing the underbelly. When you look at your company and your experience in this light, I hope that you will get many chuckles and perhaps a different perspective on your journey upwards in the company.

I first began this book in 1986 after spending many years engaging in what many people call climbing the professional ladder. My parents were particularly poor so they spent a lot of time convincing me to go to school so I didn't have to be poor like them. Like a good lad, I set my journey towards corporate life in the business world... with absolutely no idea what I was headed for. My entry into business was fairly easy as I had worked part time through university. This business world I was peeking into looked so rewarding. After all, it was the place to be. It was after graduating from university, however, that I really got immersed in this folly. And I got the bug like many others! It seemed that no matter where I was or what I was doing, there was always someone smarter, more powerful, and wealthier than me. There were also more people that seemed pretty stupid with power as well. But through my "educated" glasses it was those guys that were better than me that I needed to follow, so I began to climb in an effort to be like them. It was only logical that I should climb up the same corporate ladder that they climbed. After all, it got these guys what many strived for... more power and money.

So I climbed for some thirty years. What a struggle! Some years were great. Others were horrible. But with conviction I worked and worked, followed the rules and slowly transformed myself from technical positions in the information industry up into supervisory roles and then into management. Basically, I just followed others, took management courses and worked as hard as I could. I never questioned the process. But I noticed that not everyone worked as hard as me. Some of the guys with power and money seemed like such jerks. They didn't even seem to know what they were talking about. Yet they were feared and respected by the others... plus they made a lot of money. Was I missing something? Then, somewhere along the journey, I got to know the breed of corporate people called the "executive". These were always the golden guys that we all admired. What was so interesting about so many of these guys was that they seemed to work hard but they didn't really work... everybody else did. Was I doing something wrong? Did I go to the wrong training program? What was it that I was missing? It was only when I started to attend management and executive meetings that the secret started to reveal itself. It became apparent that many of these top leaders of corporations used many unwritten tactics to control and manipulate people. Oh yes, I will admit there are exceptions but I didn't meet many.

As I ascended the corporate ladders, I began to develop a rather oblique humorous perspective of the business world and these corporate leaders. It was here that I began to materialize a hypothesis that I dubbed as the AQ Phenomenon. Very much like the process called the "Peter Principal", the *AQ process defined how and why so many people get into disharmony with their fellow employees and how and why, despite the conflict, some still rise in status while so many others failed.* It was at that time, as Director of Information Services, that I was beginning to question my sanity and I began to look at things in a different light. The whole process of growth, promotion, career became fuzzy as I began to see conflict with the kind of person I really was. Knowing that I would have to change my personality, levels of aggression, social sphere of influence and many other individual traits if I wanted to rise farther became somewhat disconcerting. Sometimes I had to fire people, even humiliate them because they did not follow directives or rules. Sometimes I was even told by a superior that I had to treat people more horribly. What was becoming bothersome was that, as a survival tactic, I was expected to treat others like assholes or they would destroy my credibility. Even more troublesome was my changing perception of certain people in the company, and my respect for them, never mind my potential relationship with them. It was difficult to understand why so many of these people had so much power and position entrusted to them when they were really such awful jerks.

It was difficult to see how I could be part of this peculiar culture. What I observed and felt, I began to quantify in this rather obtuse process I called AQ. As I began to reflect and write about my findings I decided that I needed to get out into a new job. I decided to move to Africa and took a senior position in a new area with IBM in South Africa. You can imagine the shock. This time it took me only two years to reach another level of awareness and one of conflict with myself. The picture of what was happening was clearer now, one that allowed me to complete yet another chapter in this book. But there was still something missing... I didn't feel I had climbed high enough in the business world to give credence to my theories. So the book sat in limbo while I climbed higher in the corporate tree.

In 1988, I returned to Canada to take a Vice President position with a high tech company and truthfully forgot about my scribbling. After I became President in 1989 I began to view my interaction with people from a new level and revisited my theories, completing another chapter. When I finally gave up this position in 1997 as it was time to get out on my own as a Financial Consultant, Author and Entrepreneur. I decided to move into those positions in a quest to be free and get to a situation where no one could tell me what to do and work in my own free enterprise system. But it wasn't long before I hitched up with new partners. After being part Founder, Director, and CFO of a Private Bank in the Caribbean, then CFO of an Investment Fund Company, I realized that my hypothesis on AQ was even more relevant at the top of the heap. It didn't seem to matter what position I took, I was beholding to clients, shareholders, directors and even partners and governments who could get on my AQ list when the boom and bust cycles occurred.

Now don't get me wrong... I didn't go higher just to write a book, the idea was to attain more freedom. But this is where I became familiar with some new titles like founder, partner, director, chairman.... and so ends the story. That's where it all stopped. I could then report that I had climbed through every major step in the corporate world and beyond. In 2002, I decided it was time to share my findings and begin writing about this.

What I had determined was that employees, regardless of position, exhibit certain behaviors and characteristics that are anything but "professional". I discovered that the word organization was really a myth. The word management was really an invisible ability to collect a bunch of untaught techniques to manipulate others. I discovered that the rate of progression (or regression) in a company was actually dependant on something unexpected. The progression related to how you relate to others in the company... and more important... how you feel about them.

The whole phenomenon is wrapped up in your AQ, short for "Asshole Quotient". This is simply a measurement of your relationship to others in the company. The reality was that just about everyone in a corporation kept a secret mental list. This list contained people that they had determined were jerks... more aggressively referred to as "assholes". It is how big (or small) an individual list is relative to the individual's position in the corporation that is the crucial concern. Sound silly? Well first, let me warn you. If you are not endowed with a sense of humor about your job, or you have difficulty seeing anything amusing about corporate life, then you may not want to read this book. It may even depress you further when you realize how ridiculous we are.

Anyone who has lived in the corporate world, and I mean anyone who has worked in some organizational structure, will understand the need to grow as a professional citizen. It becomes apparent quite early in anyone's career that many traumatic experiences will be found along the way. Whether the pathway leads upwards or sideways seems to matter very little, for in either case, various rules and regulations, policies and procedures, cultures and personalities, will be encountered. These, sooner or later, will lead to disagreement or conflict. This process inevitably adds more people to the secret list. What becomes apparent is that this list is actually very important in determining how you succeed or fail in an organization. The use of this secret list is what the AQ is all about.

It is this culture, and the way companies work that is the topic here... but with a different slant than management books. Call this one "un-management" if you will... it is a look at the silly but true underbelly of a corporation. That's why I call it "Corporations Stripped Naked".

What you will read about is anything but orderly management and organizational efficiency. Rather, you will get a picture of the flip side of a company and its people. The AQ phenomenon is universal. It reveals the untaught secrets of those "successful" executives and managers. The material will vary from serious treatments to satire and exaggeration. It will inject raw humor into the grim realities of corporate life.

Special thanks are given to those many assholes I met from the past. I have met many and you are also about to meet them in this book. Some are purposely exaggerated to make a point. Thanks to them, they have made this book possible.

There is a final note here and it came about when I began to promote the book. On many interviews, after describing the AQ process, people would ask for advice on how to deal with their problems at work. This was not the intent. It was to show how people become "*Corporites*" that acquire the AQ Virus that sucks us into the mire of corporate power and need to use or abuse others. It stems from a need to preserve the ego and to protect one's position. It is something that happens to people when they engage in this Corporite addiction which is like *corporitis*, the power and preservation addiction of a very contagious virus which I call **AQ'ISM.** Once this virus takes hold you begin to lose your real personality and it becomes a *corporitic* need to survive. At the extreme, corporitis renders a company dysfunctional in what I call AQ-disequilibrium where everybody thinks everybody else is an asshole and the level of productivity (and service) infects the balance sheet, and even clients believe the company is full of assholes. That is usually bankruptcy, and I have experienced those as well.

As it turns out, to be corporitic, you need to be a dead human, like what the Corporation itself is - a dead entity for the sole purpose of engaging in commerce usually for a profit - which is without emotion or a conscience. Typically we call those beings in a corporation Assholes but it is because corporations become profitable and grow because of a dependence and interdependence on their employees. and that is where the way we do this - with or without emotion - make the big difference as to how the AQ Virus has taken hold.

This book is meant to show how employees typically take on this virus and how they shift in their corporitic behavior to become Assholes in other corporite citizens.

The big lesson here is **not** how to teach you to become an asshole addicted by ego preservation and desire for power. It is to see how the AQ Virus is caught, its symptoms, it's common behavior patterns, and to have laugh so as to avoid losing your good side of emotion and happy interrelationship in your job.

The book will refer to many of these behavior patterns as tools. I have observed these as common habits when one gets the virus. Of course to the one addicted to the power over people and the need to protect money and ego, these are tools that they use perhaps unknowingly, just like an alcoholic or smoker is unknowingly addicted to the habit.

And so, please do not seek advice on this. It is all to open your heart and avoid the AQ Virus so **you do not become** a Corporate Zombie that uses and abuses others for the sake of egoist pride and the insatiable urge to attain power over others through commerce.

When I got to the top, I found that my basic constitution was having a bad time of treating people under the spell of the virus always being ruthlessly conscious of profit, and covering my ass. I was copying what I thought was a successful formula as exhibited by the majority of corporate leaders that eventually gave me heartache and heartburn. That's why I had to exit the corporite addiction of AQ'ISM and retrench my habits.

At some point, when this happens, you need to make some serious changes to carve out a different "corporate" path.

There are always choices in these dead corporations; to engage others in a good way or a bad way. Once you see the folly of the AQ Virus, what will you choose?

Ed Rychkun

I

AQ BASICS EXPLAINED

When people join corporate structures, they must obviously learn rules, policies and procedures. They must also meet new people who begin to influence their habits and activities. Some are nice. Some are jerks. Some are smart, and some are not. Others are incompetent, while some are professional. This results in a progression where some fail badly while others succeed. Yet progression in the company seems to have little relationship to these new people's traits regardless of whether they are bad or good. For many, it becomes a mystery how they are judged. How is it that some never get promoted? How is it that some become Presidents while others remain at the bottom? How come some VP's are absolute incompetent jerks and they are still respected? What is this mysterious decision process that these corporate cultures keep within their walls?

At the base of all this is a strange culture that has people randomly failing and succeeding. There is a preoccupation with profit or some measurable means of results... a corporate performance yardstick. It is this performance yardstick and your relationship to it that has a dramatic impact on how you feel about others in the corporation.

It becomes apparent quite early in anyone's career that many traumatic experiences will be found along the way, depending on how much you contribute to the profit culture, or how well you adjust to the power hierarchy and how you measure up to this yardstick. Wherever your professional progress leads, you will always be subjected to the various rules and regulations, policies and procedures, cultures and personalities that will mystify you. These, sooner or later, will lead to "joining the fold" or "falling from the fold" and you will form an opinion about the ones that have affected you… or measured you.

Out of this process has been born a universal phenomenon that creates a preoccupation with the word asshole. Whenever a citizen disagrees with another citizen, he is quite likely to refer to him as an asshole. He can be a big one, a stupid one or a disgusting one. This relates to the size or degree. In addition, it is difficult, no matter where you are, or who you are, to at some time in your corporate career, resist the temptation of saying or thinking that disgusting word.

You may be surprised to know that you are not alone. This particular term is more universal than you can ever imagine. It is, after all, a rather effective quantification of someone else. And in its use, it happens to actually reflect the fundamental behavior and attitudes of the corporate citizens that you are trying to describe in one word… does it not? If you really look at how it is applied, it describes a universal characteristic of anyone whether a junior worker or a president.

Everyone uses the term *asshole*, some just think it, others say it. Have you ever thought "what an asshole"? And how many times have you wanted to say: *"My, my, you are a big asshole"?* Yes it's crude… but oh so descriptive! And there is a pile of emotional energy behind it! This word, and how you use it, say it, think it, quantifies how you feel about, and deal with, other people in the company. It even reflects how you treat them or how you deal with them. And it also reflects how they feel about you because that energy may be so intense, it is picked up by others. So now you come to the crux of the matter. An AQ is as quantifiable as an IQ, but much, much more revealing as you shall learn shortly.

So here is the crux. Within corporate walls, in virtually every space, there are people called employees who will, for some peculiar reason, eventually refer to each other as "assholes". Either in thought, actions, conversations, or through more esoteric communications, this colloquial terminology is eventually included in a corporate citizen's conscious space and vocabulary. Believe it or not, this is a universal habit. This preoccupation with the human posterior is not easily explained - let it be sufficient to say that it has evolved as a fairly common mental representation of someone else's qualities. This appears to be rooted in an association with some disgusting or disagreeable characteristics that the human posterior bears to someone you dislike or find disagreement with. This disagreement is, in any company, the basis for a strange phenomenon I call **AQ'ISM**. Believe it or not, even the most tight-lipped prude or the prettiest Miss Prim and Proper will eventually consider, and even utter, the word Asshole. Just ponder a while and think about how many times you've heard this expression… or may have even thought it of a fellow employee yourself? So now we have the meaning of the letter **A** in **AQ**.

Thus, when any corporate person is considered an asshole by another corporate citizen, it means that through some manner brought about by the corporate social or work mechanism, one person disagrees with, dislikes, or treats badly another within the same company.

Needless to say, the longer one associates with the same people, the more likely he or she is to become victim to this phenomenon. And quite clearly, it matters not how much one dislikes or disagrees with another, it only matters that an "asshole transformation" has occurred. Once this transformation occurs it is likely to stay. In fact, after the transformation occurs, one is likely to only add to the intensity, frequency of thought or the degree of asshole, eventually breaking down tolerance and efficiency - as we shall soon see. It is this transformation process that leads us to the concept of AQ'ISM.

AQ is short for **A**sshole **Q**uotient, which is simply the percentage of corporate citizens that any one person has converted to assholes. An AQ is therefore a personal measurement that will obviously vary from 0 (no Assholes and everybody is really nice) to 100 (everybody is an asshole - including yourself). In any company, there are a finite number of corporate citizens. For any one person, at any point in time, there will be some number of those citizens that he/she places on the asshole status list. The measurement of this state is one's AQ. It will be shown that AQ's will start at zero and increase with time - that they rarely decrease.

In general there appears to be three main interactive levels that reflect three different corporate divisions. These corporate divisions are Local (departmental), Divisional (operation, division or branch) and Corporate (head office). There appears also to be a very delicate balance between one's AQ level and one's position within these corporate groups (AQ Equilibrium). The most interesting is the Head Office or Corporate AQ. It is this AQ and the Head Office culture that we will explore in the following chapters. Before proceeding, however, let us define some fundamental laws of AQ'ISM:

1st BASIC LAW OF AQ'ISM

There exists a natural tendency within any one corporation for any one individual to classify another as an Asshole.

2nd LAW OF AQ'ISM

The percent of Assholes within any company, as viewed by any one individual at any point in time, is defined as one's Asshole Quotient or "AQ" level.

Now let us look more closely at the AQ'ISM phenomenon. When any professional or career oriented individual joins a company, his or her association with other members of the "corporate family" is minimal to non-existent. It is, in fact, quite likely that a new employee, partner or associate will be impressed with the others, otherwise joining the group would not be considered. Although exceptions may arise, for the most part, the initial contact and association is either neutral or positive. So in one's narrow little sphere, one's AQ is simply zero.... everyone is very nice, professional, smart, etc., etc.

But that sphere soon begins to grow. And, since one of the main objectives is to get along with and impress others so that one's career and subsequent rewards grow, one inevitably begins to deal with others at a more detailed level. As one settles into the company and the position, the association with others begins to broaden, as may the nature of the work. Typically one may become involved in meetings, gatherings, services, projects, verbal exchanges, or social events. Consequently, one is exposed to, and gains impressions of other's ideas, habits, opinions, capabilities and so forth. As this process continues, a person begins to phase from impressions to conclusions. As these take on a contrary nature, the result, that is one's opinion, may vary. Acceptance is a start but soon enough it may be tolerance. Or maybe disagreement prevails, perhaps even outright aggression. That is, the more one becomes exposed to other people and their ideas, the greater is the potential for disagreement.

If one gets too much of this too fast the results can be serious aggression or even depression. This has a tendency to create side effects in the form of discontentment or dissatisfaction, both of which can be recognized by others who may start to form their own opinion of the new recruit. Thus, as time ticks on, from the day of entry, as relationships, job exposure and job demands broaden, there will be a natural tendency to move new people into one's personal asshole list. Similarly, others in the company also form an impression of a new employee and, and given sufficient time, they eventually convert that person into an asshole. This conversion process whereby each can mentally convert the other is called **Interassholism**. It has some grave consequences that will be dealt with later.

In any case, consider a chronology of statements over time. It illustrates the AQ process. Imagine Barry Brass who just took a new job. These are his thoughts as he progresses in his employment:

> *"I took the job because of new opportunities and because the company is professional. I am impressed with the people."*
> *"The amount of material in this report from Sam is unreal - was it all necessary?"*

"Those three idiots in the information technology division sure are stupid."

"The office services division should be called office disservices - why doesn't the manager see how poor the service is and fire those four smart-ass typists?"

"These policies are absurd. Can't these two people realize the obvious benefits without this crap."

"The people responsible are twits - how can you get new ideas across to these two imbeciles."

"How can this Asshole give me such a poor performance review when I worked so much overtime?"

You will notice Barry's increasing aggressive and changing attitude, along with his increasing AQ. Not only is his AQ rising, so is his exposure and profile. Barry eventually converted his boss into asshole status... a fairly serious problem. Now let's look at some thoughts and statements from Barry's boss through the same period of time:

"I just hired this guy Barry Brass. He has a degree in Engineering and is as sharp as a razor - I expect him to be my right hand man."

"Barry, your evaluation of the report was quite well done but the comments on the amount of redundant information wasn't appreciated by the author."

"I will have to go down to the information technology division and tell the group that Barry was just in a bad mood - too much pressure - he didn't really mean to call the R&D group bearded weirdoes."

"Barry, why didn't you talk to me before you sent that memo about the smart ass typists?"

"These policies may be crap, but this does not mean that you can ignore a justification procedure. I suggest that you do a proper write up."

"You must do it that way, Mr. Brass, simply because I said so."

"Yes sir, I will speak with Barry, I don't think he meant to call you twits at the meeting."

"Barry, we have decided to give you no salary increase until you change your poor attitude..."

"How do I get rid of this asshole before he causes me any more trouble?"

But this is not the whole picture. There is a third side to this problem. The rest of the company that Barry is slowly getting to know is also involved in the AQ story. Some of the other people involved in Barry's corporate family are also placing him on their own AQ lists. Here are some more thoughts throughout the same period of time:

"We met Barry at the company picnic, he certainly seems to be on the ball."

"Where does this Brass kid get off telling me to take a course in writing?"

"The next time Mr. Brass excites my people this way we will have to settle the problem at the VP level."

"My wife and I met Mr. Brass at the party - he sure is a smart ass.

"You know that scum bag Brass told me I should learn how to type as fast as I gossip."

"If we don't watch out for this Brass guy we might jeopardize the project."

So Barry went merrily along slowly converting people to assholes. Not too surprising is that, given Barry's changing attitude, the boss and some other people were also converting Barry to the same status. What was happening was that Barry's AQ was rising. He started at zero and began to work diligently at increasing it over time. Now we can construct a few more simple laws.

3rd LAW OF AQ'ISM

Any new entry into a corporation will tend to have an individual AQ near zero.

4th LAW OF AQ'ISM

Any individual AQ, given sufficient time, will tend towards 100.

5th LAW OF AQ'ISM

Individual AQ's have a tendency to rise according to a natural growth process.

6th LAW OF AQ'ISM

From the date of entry into a corporation, an individual carefully sets out to prove that he or she is an Asshole.

7th LAW OF AQ'ISM

Sooner or later any individual will freely offer evidence to prove that he or she is an Asshole.

Well what does this mean? It means that people are constantly working towards becoming assholes and improving their own AQ'S. It is a natural tendency.

In further studying the AQ phenomenon, particularly as it changes in time, certain interesting observations can be made. It follows that if too many people think you are an asshole your job may be in jeopardy - you are reaching a dangerous external AQ level. Similarly, if you think too many people are assholes, *you* can approach a dangerous AQ level. Obviously, given sufficient time, your actions and opinions will become more overt. This may cause a conflict that jeopardizes your job. Although there is no hard fast rule as to what the danger level is, it is safe to say that once you reach certain levels beyond your corporate allocation, you could be in trouble and certain precautions may become necessary. This will, of course, depend upon how many immediate "bosses" are on your list and what your corporate position is. The individual allocation, called the AQ Equilibrium, will become clear later.

8th LAW OF AQ'ISM

AQ's have a tendency to be reciprocal in motion

When someone considers you an asshole, it is likely that you will feel or hear this and you feel likewise, or even stronger, about that person. This reciprocal AQ action was illustrated in the case of Barry Brass. Effectively, this process can cause assholes to be created in a chain reaction effect where one can get on someone else's AQ list without even knowing it.

Thus the AQ laws are always at work in a company of people. The fundamentals of AQ'ISM are indeed simple - just a process of converting each other to assholes. Now that we have the basics, simply think about the people you know and work with. How would you rate your AQ today?

Ok, before we move on, here is something you need to really think about when relating to the AQ process. When you first join a corporation you love everybody, right? Well, you will encounter someone who may put you off... so you may **think** that this person is an asshole. But conflicts are inevitable. If someone really puts you off or says something nasty, you may even **infer** that this person is an asshole to someone else. At some point you may let your frustrations out and **call** someone an asshole indirectly. Actually, you may find that you do not usually attain a supervisory role unless you have the "moxy" to **call** someone else an asshole. The transition to manager may actually require that you confront people directly to **tell** them they are an asshole. The next level can only be achieved by being able to **treat** others as assholes if this becomes necessary in the course of duty.

Now you are ready to see how this works in a real case.

2
THE AQ PROCESS IN ACTION

Should one study the career path of many individuals, it would be easy to see that they start somewhere in some junior position in the company. This is the first level. After some time they would attain more responsibilities and possibly some independence. In further progressing, they may deal with others outside the immediate area. They could even gain more responsibility and gain authority over others, depending upon "performance".

Similarly, the second level called management, could be achieved when new corporate players became exposed to them and judge their performance on a wider basis. The entry into the third, executive, level, would again be based upon performance with higher or more far reaching responsibilities. Moving from the bottom to the top of this pyramid requires successful movement through a corporate hierarchy through hard work and consistent performance centered at improving all that is the company. Or does it really work this way? Let us examine the AQ process and its relation to the three levels.

Wherever you go, or wherever you are, whether in a simple company with one office or a multi-national with large corporations scattered about the world, there are three main structures... executives, management and the rest. Regardless of size, some pyramid structure exists - only the titles and reporting structure becomes more complex. Thus there are three groups of people synonymous with the structure in the pyramid. There is always movement through this structure as players attempt to progress from the "lower reaches" to trample, grope and climb towards the "upper echelon".

What is significant to the AQ process is its behavior in any physical group within the overall corporate structure. This could be a head office, an operation branch, sub-office, or whatever. Each group will usually include the three levels of people, mainly the executive, middle management and the workers.

As it turns out, there are also three similar AQ levels to be aware of that correspond to position. As your AQ rises, so can your position in the pyramid. First let us look at a company called STEADFAST MEATS LTD and the AQ process as one individual Franklin P. Hardass climbs his way to the top of the pyramid. What you will see happening is a strange metamorphic process as he moves upwards.

Franklin P. Hardass is now the President and Chief Executive Officer of a large meatpacking and distribution company. He sits comfortably at the top of the pyramid in the "Upper Echelon". It took poor Frank 20 years to work his way up from the very bottom of the "Lower Reaches". He started his career when he was back in high school working in the slaughterhouse oiling mechanical equipment... not a particularly pleasant job but in those days, who could be picky?

Quite normally, when Frank started, his AQ was zero... he thought that everybody was great... the 3rd Law. All the people were hard working and he was learning incredible things from them. It was great to have a job and be part of this fantastic company and competent team. There wasn't a soul that he could say anything bad about. Frank was a fairly fast kid so it wasn't long before he learned his job fairly well, became used to his responsibilities and started to change. Frank unknowingly was to become victim to AQ'ISM. He began to notice that some of his co-workers liked to sluff off whenever possible. This started out being somewhat funny as he watched them devise ways to avoid work but it took on a more serious air when some of the slacking had a direct effect on Frank. Frank was dedicated. He did not want it to look like he was also part of this slacker's conspiracy.

Frank just worked harder and oiled more thoroughly to cover his mumblings and to cover for them. Several things were happening. Frank was changing his opinion of his co-workers. He was now bewildered about his boss being so stupid about the obvious infractions. The Basic Law of AQ'ISM was beginning to have its effect. In the meantime the co-workers began to wonder about Frank... who could be seen working after the shift to make things work. Frank and the co-workers, independently began to think about each other as not so cool... "assholes" so to speak. The reciprocal AQ Law Number 7 was now working.

Not too unpredictably, Frank's local AQ began to rise as the situation continued. Even though he didn't say too much, he began to convert his co-workers into a bunch of assholes. So far, Frank was a bit apprehensive to say anything for fear that he would get someone annoyed at him so his grumbling velocity increased.

As it turns out, Frank was learning loads of new stuff from his Mechanical Engineering course. He began to pay more attention to some of the activities surrounding the equipment. He noted that some of the co-workers must have lost all their marbles to be doing some of the things he saw. And some actually got hurt and couldn't come to work. Then Frank did something new. He

suggested to some that they were a bit stupid - that they should watch the equipment. Now Frank was operating under Law 5. He wasn't just **thinking** that they were assholes, he was beginning to **infer** that they were assholes. He suggested that they should watch the equipment more carefully

and move in only when the large mechanical arm retracted - this would save the company time and money, he said. Well this time

Frank just annoyed more of the other workers - who the hell did this oiler think he was - telling people how to do their job? Frank finally went to his boss and told him that he had some ideas that would improve the efficiency of the equipment and work place. It might even get rid of some of those

"useless assholes" as he called them.

Since the boss was a bit of a wimp when it came to dealing with people, Frank's suggestions were an opportunity to delegate, so he put Frank in charge of the oilers and set up a special project to try out the ideas. Well, needless to say, Frank now had to tell a few oilers to "get their stuff together" or "hit the road". Frank's AQ was rising. He was now **telling** people they were Assholes.

And Frank's device worked. He realigned the arm and lifted it out of the way, making it less dangerous and improving its speed. This process not only improved the mechanism, it prevented new injuries thereby increasing labor utilization. It wasn't long before the Plant Manager got wind of this so when Frank's boss retired, Frank was a natural for the supervisor's job. Now Frank was in charge. "*This guy has balls*", said the manager, "*we need people with balls.*" Now Frank could **call** many more people slackers and assholes any time he wanted to - directly to their faces! His AQ was rising rapidly but this was fine since his stature was also rising.

Then a new encounter occurred. Frank's boss, Sam Suckhole, an insipid runt of a man, controlled the packing and butchering divisions as well as the slaughter division. One day while Frank was walking

through packing, he noticed piles of boxes thrown about between the conveyors. Feeling in a helpful mood he walked over to Bill Blastoff, the packing supervisor and said *"Bill, these boxes are dangerous, you ought to clean them up before someone gets hurt. You should tell those boxers not to make such a mess."*

The comment just didn't get taken in the right context. Frank not only irritated Bill but a few of the boxers heard him so the topic at coffee break was obvious.

"Who the hell is this Franklin Asshole?" they muttered, "Where does he get off telling us what to do?" This only gave Bill more fuel for the fire. The next thing that happened was that Frank's boss, Sam Suckhole, called him in the next day to ask about his encounter with the Packing Department. *"Look Frank"*, he said, "*packing is not your concern, so keep your nose out of there unless you are*

asked!" Guess what was happening to Frank's AQ? And guess what was happening with Frank's stature on other AQ lists?

Frank was infuriated and steamed back to his office to sketch out a memo to Herbert Hoyle, the Plant Manager. Then he walked into the Plant Manager's office with it. *"Mr. Hoyle,"* he said, *"I*

have produced a memo to formally identify a terrible inefficiency. To summarize, there are ten points. First, the Packing Department is dumping boxes all over the floor between conveyors. This is a hazard to maintenance as well as workers. They are also producing excessive boxes beyond the packing capacity. This means they may have too many boxers. It also means they are using excessive space which could be used for conveyor expansion. Why not get rid of some of these jerks, save money, be more productive and provide space for expanding the conveyor system? The possibilities of improvement are vast..."

Herb interrupted Frank, "Hold on Frank, slow down a minute... let me read your memo and get back to you this afternoon." Guess what? A meeting was scheduled for the next day, with Frank making a presentation. Bill Blastoff, Sam Suckhole and Herb Hoyle were told to be there, along with the Vice President Earl Klutz who just happened to be visiting Hoyle on a plant tour.

By this time it will be noted that Frank has increased his sphere of influence from a local to a divisional level. Not only that, he was now dealing with middle management, a completely new group of characters. Even Frank's boss was involved in the AQ program. Now he was really cheezed off because Frank had ignored his advice to mind his own business.

At the meeting Frank tried to be cool and he just presented the facts as he saw them. Bill Blastoff and Sam Suckhole were asked to comment on their lack of movement on the issue. While Earl Klutz sat quietly, Bill raged and Sam said it was a good idea, he just hadn't had the time to activate similar measures.

Well the fact that Sam had just been telling Herb how efficient the boxing operation was didn't help the situation. It didn't take long - the next day in fact, to move Sam into the cattle warehouse as Senior Advisor to the Steer Manure Disposal Task Force. And Frank was promoted to Manager in Sam's place.

Through the next year, there wasn't a mess that Frank didn't catch and raise hell about. Everybody came to know Franklin as he thundered through the plant. He was dedicated to raising his AQ. He wasted no time telling people that sloppy workers were not going to be part of his team.

Herbert Hoyle moved on to head office since there seemed to be so many improvements at the plant. Earl Klutz then made Frank the Plant Manager. Now there weren't many people left to get on the local AQ list. At some point Frank had an encounter with each and every one of the plant people.

He had either **told** them directly they were an Asshole and better shape up, or he had **treated** them like an Asshole. Frank was at the top of the heap. His AQ had risen but his position in the company was also rising.

But the story doesn't stop here. Frank began to meet a new breed of people at the Plant Manager's meetings. He began to encounter the head office breed. By now Frank had become involved in other areas such as administration, finance, marketing and so on - most of which he knew very little about. But that didn't matter to Frank… at least at the plant level. *"Beefs beef and everybody eats,"* he used to say, *"why make a big deal about marketing? An efficient plant is where it's at!"*

This attitude eventually got Frank into trouble at a general meeting oriented towards a marketing strategy. Now Frank was rubbing shoulders with the executive level from head office. Frank's new era started at one of the meetings where he was making his usual statements about beef when Slink Wirlwind, the VP of Marketing took exception to the comment. Slink had just given a short presentation stating that consumer prices were falling at 15%. When Frank made the comment about marketing, Slink immediately asked Frank to present his strategy for a 15% revenue increase next year. Not only did Frank put Slink on his AQ list, but he ended up looking like a bit of a boisterous idiot to the others who chuckled to themselves quietly.

Frank vowed to redeem his prestige and went home quietly - licking his wounds. *"I'll fix that bastard,"* he muttered. *"I'll show the Asshole how to increase revenue!"*

Frank was merciless when it came to cutting costs and keeping people in line. Not surprising, the plant ended up producing a better profit than other plants, despite prices. Frank had no problems pointing this out at all the inter-division meetings, each time modifying his AQ. In the meantime, the plant was creaking with tension. Labor unrest, deteriorating equipment, and new issues were beginning to surface. But so what? Frank was making the company a lot of money.

Through a few more meetings, Frank learned to be careful about what he said. Not only did he pick up some of the executive tricks, he had had a chance to take several courses on tactics, presentations and a course on "The Practice of Hedging on the Futures Market". Finally Frank was invited to a meeting at head office where some discussion was to take place on the crisis of falling prices and the affect on the next year's profits. Frank was ready - he would just wait for Slink to screw up.

About one hour into the meeting, Slink was laying out where future sales would come from. *"We are rapidly moving into an age of meatball mania,"* he said smugly, *"we have done a psychological profile analysis of high school graduates. Conclusively they say that they have just begun to appreciate the* importance of meatballs instead of chicken burgers and expect them to play an important part of their lives. Without a shadow of a doubt," he grinned with cool arrogance, "we must direct our marketing energies towards all retail outlets which have any capabilities for distributing meatballs.... all our research and projections indicate a possible unprecedented growth. Perhaps," he said, "you gentlemen have some ideas?"

This was Frank's queue - he had it in for Slink anyway. "Mr. Wirlwind" he said as he stood up, "we are currently sitting in a situation where falling prices are shrinking profits quickly and where plant and operating efficiencies must play a vital role in securing more profit regardless of price. We have seen during the last year how my plant has, through attention to this basic

principle, produced more profit than all others put together. Rather than dream about teenage consumers, we should attend to the reality of the present..." Slink was shocked and stood up in anger. "And what is your miracle plan Mr. Hardass?" he asked wryly.

Remembering his Commodity Hedging course, Frank said "One of the most effective means of preserving capital and profits is through the hedging mechanism by clearly selling forward cattle, hogs and pork bellies, then buying back at anticipated lower prices or delivering the commodity which we have at our Ranching Operations. This has the effect of locking in profits even if prices decrease, as you and our VP of Finance, Mr. Dancer knows." Turning to the President, Frank continued his pitch. "Thus, in my estimation, we should have the marketing *division concerning themselves with anticipated price trends and educating themselves in hedging techniques, rather than doing surveys on meatballs...."*

Frank quite elegantly succeeded in doing several things. He got back at Slink for making him look stupid on plant efficiency. He took a good shot at Slink and his department and positioned himself as superior. And, he brought out a new idea. To top it, he even took a shot at Scab Dancer in Finance. Well, the air was thick with smoke and the silence was frightening as AQ counters clicked away. Finally the president said, *"Frank, how do you propose we can take advantage of this and what is the cost?"* So the meeting shifted focus to Frank and a simple idea. Fortunately for Frank, he had learned to delegate almost anything he knew nothing about, just like the others in the meeting.

He simply went to the board and showed with some simple price changes in one year what the impact would be, depending upon the resulting projections, which he said, must be the responsibility of good market analysts. He said the costs of execution were trivial since all principles, and staff, were already in place.

IT IS DIFFICULT TO CONVEY TO ALL YOU EXECUTIVE ASSHOLES THE MAGNITUDE OF YOUR STUPIDITY

It didn't take Frank very long to become the Vice President of Operations. Frank had also learned to do something new - he could actually **tell** someone senior he was an Asshole and then **treat** him like one - right out in the open. Now as VP of Operations, Frank dealt directly with new people at a different level. He could now call in all plant managers and tell

35

them they were assholes when profits dropped. He could threaten the new plant manager at the operation that he had almost destroyed through his ferocious and merciless price-cutting... absolving him of any past problems.

Frank worked diligently on his new level of AQ as he moved up the executive ladder. Note that not only was Frank's AQ rising steadily but so was his position in the pyramid. Frank was getting to be so powerful that he could treat people like assholes without even knowing it. He could just send a memo around and reach people he had never met. It would only be a matter of time before Frank would learn to treat everyone like an asshole and win his way to the presidency.

And therein was the grand finale of Frank's climb to the upper echelon. Only when Frank knew that he was also an asshole, and would enter his own AQ list could he really be at the top, with an AQ score of 100.

What is illustrated here is a fairly normal progression through a company. Although Frank climbed all the way, many only climb part of the way. Nevertheless, the climbing process is the same. Even in the case where one "job hops" the process is still the same. An AQ just behaves differently. In any case, Frank moved upward through the three levels, from worker, through management to executive, each time raising his AQ as he went through successive positions.

Each succession had more responsibility (affecting more people) and each time he encountered wider scope (dealing with new people and larger problems). Frank, quite simply, went from the lower reaches (worker) through middle management (doers) to the executive (decision makers) as he went through a very systematic metamorphosis up an AQ progression.

At each step, Frank met newer and more influential people in the organization. At each phase he had to impress someone or show results by out-performing something or someone. This was typically done at the expense of the AQ as it rose higher and higher at each encounter. In each step, Frank could influence more and more people, effectively treating them like assholes, without even knowing it. Eventually, of course, there would be fewer and fewer people left. Indeed, Frank had moved from the lower reaches as a common worker, through middle management and into the executive echelon of the company by successfully raising his AQ as he climbed.

But there is another major point to this story. If you look at the 20 years it took Frank to ascend, you find that the actual crucial events that made the difference in the climb were quite few and far between. The situations, and the total elapsed time were in fact minute compared to the whole time span. The vast majority of time was spent just doing a job. Sure Frank needed some basic skills, but the bottom line was that he was moved upwards because he kept his AQ in line with his position. Before I explain this, we need to try to quantify this peculiar process.

3

MEASURING YOUR AQ

We can now consider representing the 5th Law of AQ'ISM as a physical process. The law, which states, "*Individual AQ's have a tendency to rise according to a natural exponential growth*

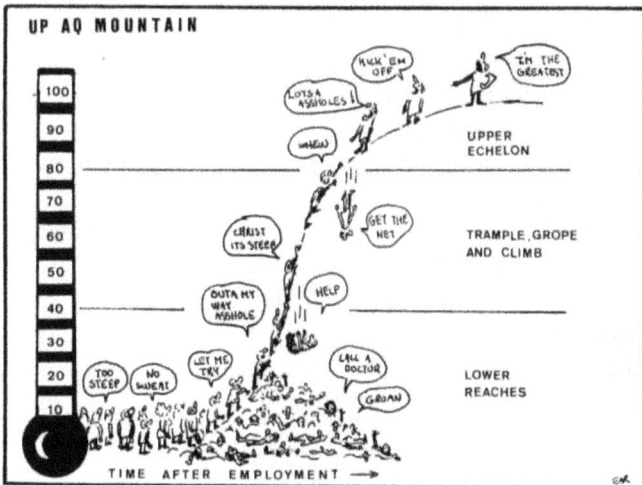

THE AQ CLIMB - UP AQ MOUNTAIN

process" is represented in the figure. The AQ starts low and slow because one takes a bit of time to learn the job and the corporate family. Quite obviously it must end slow because there are fewer and fewer people to convert to assholes. In between, as one's sphere of influence changes, and relations or responsibility increase, the AQ moves quite swiftly. During the middle management time, it is amazing how fast you can make the AQ rise. But the climb gets steeper and harder.

If we can recall Franklin's story, we see that he moved through several phases of stature but if you noted his changing attitude you would notice six AQ phases:

1. he began to **THINK** that some co-workers were assholes
2. he started to **INFER** that others were assholes
3. he gained courage to **CALL** others assholes directly
4. he began to **TELL** people that they were assholes
5. he started to **TREAT** people as assholes indirect and direct
6. he knew he had to **BE** an asshole himself to succeed

Notice how (ironically) you accept you must become an asshole yourself if you are to succeed at the top! This particular sequence, identifying how Frank interacted with others, has a direct correlation with the level of aggression, power, and position. We will identify these as the "AQ METER" phases. The AQ METER identifies the successive transformation process of creating assholes. Regardless of whether you treat, tell, call, infer, or think, the end result is the same - you have created an asshole in some way or other. What is important to the individual's corporate growth is the particular sequence of AQ phases. This metamorphic process from when you first "think asshole" to when you become one must be carried out in careful order - in conjunction with the AQ number.

In following the career path or professional progression of an employee it is obvious that he must move from a potential "nobody", through various supervisory levels, management and possibly into the executive. This will depend upon where the employee enters the company. One of the important ingredients in this progression is related to the AQ-METER and the level that one has achieved. And how does one achieve a new level? Well, here is what it appears to reduce to. One does not usually attain a supervisory role unless he has the "moxy" to **call** someone else an asshole. Right? Or more appropriately convey to his superior that someone or something is wrong, can be improved upon, etc. The transition to Manager, however, requires that one must be able to confront people directly, to **tell** or prove another's unworthiness should disciplinary measures be required.

The next level can only be achieved by being able to **treat** others as assholes if this becomes necessary in the course of duty. Now bear in mind that this does not mean that you always need to be a negative jerk, you just need to show the superiors that you are able to handle conflict by being "tough" if you need to be. The truth is that we all like to be "team players" and "coaches" or "leaders", not jerks. But when the shit hits the fan and all that great team stuff doesn't work, what does management resort to? A team whistle? Hardly. They need to build on their ability to climb up the AQ Meter. It should be noted that the AQ climb upwards normally requires firstly accomplishing each previous phase of thinking, inferring, calling, telling and treating... without skipping any one phase.

The metamorphic phases of thinking, inferring, calling, telling, treating, and being are illustrated in the picture.

THINK

INFER

CALL

TELL

TREAT

ARE

If you find this hard to believe, think about a new employee walking around calling people assholes. His career is in immediate danger. Or think about the wimpy manager who is afraid to tell people they are assholes because they were over budget. His career may also be in danger. And how many vice presidents would retain their positions if they were not able to treat people like assholes if they needed to? In fact, one must successively show an ability to work well with one phase before being allowed to activate the next.

There are three levels to be aware of. In the first level, as a worker, Frank set out to either disagree with or irritate co-workers in his department and even got into trouble with his superiors. His local AQ, if computed on the basis of total department workers, was, needless to say, maximized. In the next segment of his life, when he moved from supervisor to plant manager, and into the middle management category, he had new people to piss-off or disagree with. The situation was a bit different, however, in that he was working at a higher level and could affect more people at one time. In fact Frank could hold a meeting and piss off a whole group at one time simply because he was not happy with something and told them so. Frank's next level occurred when he moved to head office as VP Operations and into the executive level.

Again he could deal with new people and make even wider-reaching decisions. Now Frank could just send a memo to all divisions and treat huge numbers of people like assholes without even seeing them. One memo, if carefully worded by an asshole could effectively get the whole company on the AQ list! In each of the three levels Frank would have a limited number of people to place on his list and therefore he would eventually maximize his AQ in each of the three levels. Since the overall AQ is cumulative, AQ saturation is possible within any one spatial location. That is, if you work in an isolated group there are only so many people you have contact with, even though there are many more people in the company. Conversely, as you move into the executive, there are more and more people you can affect without even knowing them.

So out of this can be created another AQ Law.

The 9th LAW OF AQ'ISM :

Your local AQ will rise to its level maximum within a period of 2 years.

Now this one is odd in that there appears to be an average time period within which an AQ can rise to dangerous levels. This means that if you take work in a particular department or localized group it will take 2 years to get most of the group on your AQ list. Six months to do the job well, six months to figure out what to disagree with, six months to get the courage to change that which you disagree with and six months to reap some benefits. Every step takes its toll on the AQ list. So what do you do when everyone in the group is on your list... including your boss? Well, if you become the boss you may be ok but if you're not, you are in **AQ Disequilibrium** and you may be headed for trouble! The whole process is cumulative and it is difficult to escape it unless you move to a new company.

If you should join a company at a junior level and begin by calling others assholes, you would have missed two steps and could be terminated quite easily. In other words, you would not have conditioned your audience properly by going through the lower steps. Any attempt to miss steps on the ladder can quite easily result in falling off into the lower reaches. The net result could be to get fired or displaced (as Sam Suckhole did) to useless senior positions or to just become a general nobody who could only think, infer or maybe even indirectly call others assholes. These failure cases will be fearful of trying anything higher on the AQ ladder. These people are a special class of workers because they are in "AQ Disequilibrium". This is where the position is lower than the AQ suggests it should be.

We can now create an "AQ METER". This meter tells you what AQ Level you should be at given any particular position. Conversely, knowing what your AQ is should indicate the level and position you should be at. An interesting aside is that you cannot usually jump steps unless you have come into the position from outside. It should then take 2-3 years to reach a state of AQ-Equilibrium.

THE ASSHOLE METER

LEVEL	STATE	AQ	METHOD	PROCESS
DECISION MAKERS	PRESIDENT	100	ARE	Rule
UPPER ECHELON	VICE PRESIDENT	90		Power
		80	TREAT	Superiority
DOERS	DIRECTOR	70		Control
MIDDLE MANAGEMENT	MANAGER	60	TELL	Conflict
	SUPERVISOR	50		Change
		40	CALL	Responsibility
WORKERS	SENIOR	30		Confidence
	INTERMED	20	INFER	Exposure
LOWER REACHES	JUNIOR	10		Learning
	NOBODY	0	THINK	Impressions

Finally, we have the 10th Law:

THE 10th LAW OF AQ'ISM

Your level of responsibility must rise in direct relationship to your AQ level.

Now, let us find out what happens when you violate some of these equilibrium laws.

4

EFFECT OF AQ'ISM ON PRODUCTIVITY

In the previous section we saw how the AQ Meter phases of think, infer, call, tell and treat were key factors in a natural progression into management and executive levels. Thus, there was a direct relationship between the AQ, the phases and the corporate position. A mismatch is known as **AQ-Disequilibrium.**

As an AQ reaches higher levels, a very dangerous situation exists when the position in the company is not equally as high. Remember that it is high because you disagree with or don't like someone else and that this is more than likely a reciprocal arrangement. Moreover, it may be high because you have treated others badly, sometimes unknowingly. Remember also that an asshole, once converted, becomes difficult to convert back. When an AQ reaches great heights, it may become very easy to get fired or laid off, or even receive lateral to lower demotions. Needless to say, if you don't like a lot of people, your dislike cannot be hidden for long and eventually pressure will come to bear upon you, particularly if your position is not lofty enough to allow such prerogatives.

It is at this point that your survival will depend upon your skills, and your position. This will determine your progression (or regression) to a new position. Paradoxically, those who do not make moves to disagree with or do not become forceful with others in an outward manner, will not progress into upper management. Recall how Frank took certain initiatives to create assholes? Are these assholes not your paving stones to progress?

In AQ Equilibrium, as the AQ and position increase, so does productivity. If any mismatching occurs there can be a negative impact on productivity so the converse occurs where efficiency *decreases* as the AQ increases. In this respect, various crisis points are evident along the AQ Meter, particularly at points of transition between management levels. First let me explain productivity.

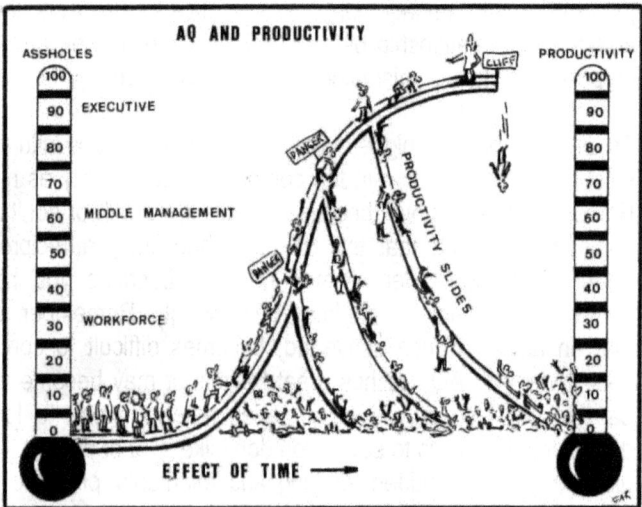

AQ EFFECT ON PRODUCTIVITY – DOWN AQ MOUNTAIN

Quite clearly upon employment, one's time is spent in activities of "learning the ropes" and meeting people, rarely interfering with another's productivity or work habits. Upon learning one's job and being exposed directly to other's work, one can go through a period of increasing his productivity quite substantially. There comes a time where familiarity of the tasks performed, knowledge of other's work, and exposure to methods will result in some form of criticism, or disagreement that may result in a betterment of production. If the employee does not get his way in such matters he may become disgruntled, lose respect, and, of course, become less productive. Recall Frank's progression?

In further carrying on this scenario, the new ideas and work efficiency will affect the judgment of the employee's competency and promotion. Changes to existing systems usually mean, however, that someone else or someone else's ideas need modification and this can result in considerable conflicts (higher AQ). It then becomes necessary that one must be able to convince or sway others to precipitate a change that will increase production.

Failure results in a lack of promotion and further disgruntlement, thus further lowering productivity. It is at these failure points that AQ and productivity can diverge rapidly. Effectively, one can be busy fighting, convincing, writing, etc., to better things, raising AQ quickly with each encounter, yet spend less time being directly productive. Passing through this phase will be at another's expense and will depend upon the individuals' tenacity in convincing others. Look back at the picture of AQ and productivity. Notice those productivity slides that come swooshing down? That's what happens to one's productivity in these cases.

In fact, productivity begins to be measured on the basis of how quickly one can effect change. Eventually the individual will have to gain wider exposure, taking more and more responsibility for a certain function, department, etc. and begin to control people, processes and money directly or indirectly. More and more emphasis is placed upon effective direction, supervision and management of people and production processes. The next phase depends upon the ability, again, to precipitate change but at a greater or higher level. That is, more and more people/processes are affected and entirely new areas, or methods or projects must be exploited to the good of the company. Anyone who has shown ability to manage people, projects or processes effectively is a candidate for greater things. He must, however, be able to seek out and exploit new and profitable opportunities for the company. This rather idealistic scenario describes the transition of an individual from the workforce through middle management into the executive.

Now what we have described is a **Worker** who has undergone a change into a **Doer** who has changed into a **Decision Maker**. Each transition marks a potential crisis point where very opposite effects can occur in terms of productivity. If failures occur which deny movement from **Worker** to **Middle Management** or into **Executive**, a drastic change in productivity can occur. Needless to say the higher up the AQ METER this occurs, the greater the affect on company productivity and the individual.

As a worker, productivity increases by learning and doing a special task or tasks well, possibly modifying tasks to be more efficient. As a middle manager, productivity increases by better control, direction and motivation of people. This then would create a more efficient process. As an executive, productivity increased by new acquisitions or major changes as related to new or existing opportunities, directions or processes. The evaluation and assessment capability would be highly important to affect production and profits.

As this process continues it should be kept in mind that one is battling the PETER PRINCIPLE and failures along the way become bigger and more devastating to both company and personal confidence. Thus, several major failure points are most common, as shown in the previous figure on AQ Productivity. These were the productivity slides mentioned earlier.

The effect on personal or company productivity is obvious depending upon where one got to before the slide downwards.

In looking at these failure or crisis points, at the three levels, negative efficiencies are created as:

- More and more time is spent criticizing people or work, bothering others and causing trouble.
- More and more time is required to motivate people, to maintain existing production levels and to convince people of change.
- Criticism, antagonism and subjective emotional meetings are common - resulting in a lack of control.
- More and more time is spent in meetings arguing about opportunities and useless details.
- Personality disputes interfere with decisions that could improve company profits or opportunities.
- Blaming others is common.

High AQ's have a tendency to become more destructive over time. The absolute extremes include a dictatorship with power or a babbling idiot without power. Even worse is a senile old has-been with power. As mentioned before, through the phenomenon of inter-assholism any company can ultimately achieve a state of ASSHOLE SATURATION where everybody thinks, infers, tells or treats everybody else as assholes. This state becomes fairly evident when employee turnover is slight, giving everybody sufficient time to get to the infer, tell and call levels of the AQ

METER but not having enough promotions to go around. The result is failures, disgruntlements, discontent and diminishing productivity. In fact after a few years, people assume seniority and begin to:

- believe that menial tasks are below them
- do just enough to get by until a promotion appears
- believe they are independent thinkers and that the method of doing a job is up to them alone
- believe that they alone are experts
- become protective about their positions and prior decisions
- take more advantage of the company in terms of expenses, liberties
- spend more time in discussions about other's affairs and company politics
- become mo
- re concerned about job security than job efficiency

ASSHOLE SATURATION

It is easy to see that the above can easily create too many "bosses", poor motivation, lack of control, disorganization and decreasing productivity. Such environments become very depressing as tyrants and powerful imbeciles attempt to control complainers, slackers, and unproductive people with a deluge of ever increasing rules, policies and general administrivia. The stupidity of the situation is that everybody thinks that they are great and that the other guy is the incompetent asshole. What really happens is that everybody just becomes a bigger asshole to the other guy - but we will examine this in a separate section.

So contrary to normal corporate rules of hiring for long times, minimizing staff turnover, it may be desirable to encourage the opposite, thus avoiding Asshole Saturation. The whole process, once entrenched, will eventually collapse the company given any economic change. In good times, there is room, profit and potential for all, and saturation continues unattended and unnoticed. But just imagine how productive the situation is in the example above. Like Government?

5

THE CORPORATE HIERARCHY

Once an individual has entered another's asshole list it is because he has progressively set out to do so, even if it is unknowingly. Corporations are essentially governed by the profit motivation (i.e. generate profit) and as such, tend to guide its citizens through policies, rules, behavior, ideologies, etc. that create a "corporate culture" focused on that mandate. Not surprising, this creates a prototype behavior in those that take on this mandate. Oddly enough the most successful members develop some predictable characteristics that the followers, or status climbers, attempt to copy.

Thus laws, policies and behavioral "ethics" either guide, police or "motivate" citizens in those directions that are supposed to be good for the company. They are designed to protect the company, or allow progress, maintain profits, and so on. I am sure you have heard all this before. It is for the "good of the company" of course!

Undoubtedly this is why executives wear slick suits, people have to come to work at certain times, levels of authority are defined, reporting is strict, and so on. But the most important notion is that work must get done within the corporate rules and products must be produced. *Everybody* is supposed to do this in efficient ways that maintain or increase profits.

This underlying mission does different things to different people. Call it a penguin or lemming mentality if you will but such forced behavior has a tendency to generate prototype assholes that, like in any culture, have good and bad components. The fact is, however, within a corporate culture, your success within it will typically depend upon how good a producer you are in following the mandate. If you recall Frank's progression in life, his greatest steps in the climb came when he was able to produce something... more of it, better than before, or propose ways to improve things. After all, this is the usual trade for position, power and money, right?

Clearly you need to keep this mission in your mind if you want to move upward. You must be able to either directly or indirectly improve profit. The more opportunities you locate that show this to others above you, the better opportunity you have to climb. Unfortunately this may mean increasing the AQ to tromp on those poor souls who are in the path of your merciless climb to increased productivity. That's corporate life whether we like it or not. The typical successful prototype, therefore, must dispense with emotion and be logical. He must always seek out and take advantage of opportunities. He must be able to exploit situations to the betterment of the company. Whether situations or people are involved matters not, for he must be strong, forceful and confident. He must PRODUCE! This is a good theory but in practice most are not able to do this. The smart prototype is selective, finding occasional time to make the move, works consistently on his AQ and makes a move when the AQ is reaching disequilibrium. The rest of the time, he simply coasts, and uses special tools to not only maintain his AQ, but to maintain the position. Frank did just this, and he needed only a handful of key situations in the twenty years to do this.

Productivity is different dependant on the level in the organization... and in particular, the level of AQ. Let us summarize the three main levels and what productivity means at each stage.

As a **WORKER**, productivity increases with learning and doing special functions, usually in *conjunction with others.* Movement to the next levels will depend upon how well this is done.

As a **MANAGER**, productivity increases are *through others*. That is, better control, direction, motivation of people, functions or processes.

As an **EXECUTIVE**, productivity increases will again be through others but more commonly *using* (we call it leading or directing) *others.* Major changes, directional missions, new opportunities, for example, are imposed on others to attain new heights in productivity, profit, and so on.

The bottom line is that we must first work with others, then through others and then use others in order to continue to be productive. If not, remember the productivity slides? This business becomes quite easy if you understand this process and develop a few critical abilities that we will dub as the **AQ Rules of Conduct. This typically what happens to conduct:**

- People learn to create assholes with a cold, logical and emotionally detached attitude - in accordance with the AQ METER.
- People learn to apply the AQ Phases of think, infer, call, tell, treat at the right time, in synch with the AQ meter.

- People learn to use others well - call it motivation or whatever - but get them to produce more by paying attention to the AQ.
- People learn to strike quickly when there is a chance to increase productivity and increase AQ.
- People learn how to seek and exploit opportunities even if it means destroying opposition at their expense.

Now I didn't say that this is right. I just say this is the way it is most of the time. You can dream about being the prefect employee, or top producer all you like but if you happen to encounter someone in tune with these rules you will be "dethroned" faster than you would like to think. Needless to say, your strength of character, ability to find opportunities and your killer instincts for destroying opponents will help you carry out the above rules. The use of these "rules" affects your climb up the corporate tree. At each branch on the tree is an employee upon whom you must apply one of the rules to climb higher. The easiest way to climb over one is to convert him to an asshole. Pretty disgusting isn't it?

It goes without saying that this culture has a tendency to create certain prototypes with fairly common characteristics simply because the "rules of the game" become fairly universal. After all, if you can progress up the ladder faster, why bother with all the school taught fairyland stuff? I have seen Harvard Business graduates get unseated rapidly by someone skilled in AQ conduct rules. And your success will depend upon how well you have learned and played them out. They are not taught in business school. The best players are those with special instincts to play this rather obtuse game.

Well, the whole process of corporate cultures, their rules and purposes creates typical predictable plastic prototypes.

Whereas, it is more difficult to depict the WORKERS in prototype moulds, it becomes easier to do this as they progress up the ladder because each step means that more and more rules have been learned and played. The process is no different than a football team - they all look the same and start without position (particularly from a distance), they must play according to the rules but each has a varying degree of skill or strength in performing within these rules and positions.

In the corporation the skill and strength whereby you play the AQ game leads to profit and power.

If all this is becoming too depressing and serious, one should think about the corporate culture as a tree, upon which birds perch and above which they fly. In fact the analogy to the bird kingdom is quite interesting. If you don't believe this, consider whether it is corporate player or bird we speak of in the following:

- they have a tendency to shit indiscriminately upon others lower down
- they have a greater shit impact depending upon the height achieved
- they look silly and lose status when they lose their cover
- they attempt to fly higher than others to seek new territory or victims
- the higher they fly the more powerful they must be
- they depend upon preying on other's misfortunes
- their survival instincts must be highly developed to become big and fat
- their mobility/strength dictate how well they can capture territory and victims
- they make similar sounds like grunt, hoot, screech, squawk
- they can have high killer or savaging instincts

Does this sound like the group you last encountered in a corporate boardroom? There was a time that I actually saw some of these birds... and birdbrains... sitting in meetings and around boardroom tables. Many a time it took the tension off for me! I also found it pretty interesting that all these birds lose a lot of their power when they are all at the same elevation. In the tree, they can rely on their stature (elevation in the tree) but around a good rowdy session at a board meeting these birds become vulnerable and exposed. There's a tip here... if you want to execute some AQ strategies that they use; get them off their perch first! But we will learn about that later.

These characteristics identify the corporate requirements of many who seek the top positions in a company. Actually the characteristics of strength (power), mobility (seeking opportunity), and shitting (communication) are common to all, but the survival instinct or method of approach shows some variations. Two opposite methods are dominant. That is, while one type preys on fresh meat (new opportunities), the other type preys on dead meat (old opportunities). One finds new ways while the other scabs off others. It is like a positive and negative polarity. Just consider this analogy:

While one flies to seek out new victims, the other seeks out old victims. Needless to say, the higher one's position, the more one can see and strike at. This will depend upon strength and mobility. So, from the top down we identify certain birds, each with either fresh or old prey instincts and all with decreasing strength and mobility, and all being able to shit, but not necessarily upon others - you must achieve height to do so. Check out this table for example:

GROUP	FRESH MEAT	DEAD MEAT	EXAMPLE
DECISION	EAGLES	CONDORS	EXECUTIVE

MAKERS	HAWKS	VULTURES	
DOERS	OWLS FALCONS PARROTS	KITES RAVENS SEAGULLS	MIDDLE MANAGEMENT
WORKERS	TURKEYS CHICKENS	OSTRICHES PENGUINS	WORK FORCE

Now if this looks pretty silly, just think about the key characteristics of these birds. Starting from the bottom up:

CHICKENS or PENGUINS are essentially flockers or like to stick together. They make much noise, can be herded easily and simply make a lot of mess. The difference between the two is that one has some economic value (positive worker), in that it can be eaten and produces food, whereas the other (negative worker) is of little economic value. Both are easily preyed upon and both shit and squawk. Neither can fly above the other, as a matter of fact, they can't even fly!

TURKEYS or OSTRICHES Moving up a bit now, we have a bit of economic significance (meat in the turkey) but we are still looking at moderate flockers. There is less economic significance with the ostrich (negative) and he has a tendency to bury his head in the sand, ignoring reality. Note that they are larger in size and more difficult to prey upon but still cannot fly.

PARROTS or SEAGULLS Now we have a new dimension - that of flight – and being able to achieve height. Secondly, there is a stronger tendency to seek food more aggressively and individually. Both, although mobile, are squawkers but gulls are more likely to live off of waste. Their economic significance has become minimal.

FALCONS or RAVENS Mobility has increased as has the tendency towards individuality and self-survival. The economic significance begins to show through as being able to seek new areas for food. The raven, however, is more of a scavenger rather than a swift attacker of live prey.

OWLS or KITES Somewhat stronger, mobility is higher with the added advantage of owls being able to kill at night, thus increasing their horizons for opportunity. The kite, however, although swift, relies on stealing from others.

HAWKS or VULTURES Hawks can fly higher and are larger and stronger. They are swift and dangerous, easily covering vast areas to seek and kill within. Vultures are more likely to seek out dead carcasses even though they are large and quite mobile.

EAGLES or CONDORS These are the ultimate in strength, danger and height attainment. They, like Hawks and Vultures, are capable of adequately demolishing those below. They can soar higher and longer. Again, one is a scavenger while the other is not.

So the higher you can get, the more you can shit on (get the AQ up fast) poor unsuspecting people.

- The faster you are, the easier you can escape and the faster you can kill.
- The bigger you are the less likely you are to get eaten and the more able you are to eat or tromp someone else.
- The higher you can fly, the more areas you can exploit.

But at the very bottom of the tree are a couple more species that the ones above don't ever talk about but nevertheless think about. These are the employees that will never bother to climb the tree, don't care to be part of the whole show and they probably don't have the ability to do so. These people can only "think" others are assholes. Many never dare to indulge in the other phases and typically hang around at the bottom of the tree. For some higher up, such people are just necessary bottom feeders and are pretty awful creatures. You now have a complete picture of the corporate hierarchy and the tree. Check out the next page.

UP THE CORPORATE TREE – THE HIERARCHY

In the corporate tree family, there are what I refer to as **Grunts**. Why? Well because that's typically how they talk. And when they do, that appears to be a direct relationship to their level of IQ... not AQ! Grunts are fairly immobile creatures that simply crawl around in the debris at the bottom. It is not that this is so bad. It is just the way it is.

Now how does this all relate to the AQ METER and the corporate scenario? Look again at the picture of the corporate tree and its residents shown on the previous page.

We see that there are both positive and negative (predatory and scavenging) members in the corporate family. And once they get into the tree, they look pretty good, despite their positive or negative use of the Rules of Conduct, or despite some of their vile habits.

In fact, many do appear this way to others and certainly this is the way they may appear to themselves. Well this is definitely not the way others always see our lofty tree dwellers as we shall see in the next section.

Let me leave you with this picture in your mind for a while.

6

AQ DIS-
EQUILIBRIUM

In the previous section we looked at the corporate tree with its earthy and lofty dwellers. In reality, the vast majority of corporate citizens remain below the tree. As others climb the tree then fall, their productivities fall. Additionally, through the inter-assholism effect, they may view each other in ever changing perspectives.

In real life only a select few can climb their way upwards at the same pace as their AQ. There can only be so many supervisors, managers, vice presidents, etc., in any company. But what happens to the others? Obviously they are in AQ-DISEQUILIBRIUM! People fall off the AQ ladder constantly but this doesn't drop their AQ - it can even climb faster depending upon how disgruntled one is from the fall. Have you ever seen a happy demoted employee? Or how about one who hasn't been promoted while his co-workers were? What about those who have received poor evaluations and no wage increases? These people think just about everybody is an asshole. Even the guy who got caught feeling up the cleaning lady quickly converted everyone who found out about it.

So despite corporate positions, AQ's still continue to forge ahead, even accelerating when the disequilibrium gap is wide. It has been stated that once a conversion does take place, the process is virtually irreversible. That is, there is such a thing as a corporate memory that doesn't forget, so an asshole once created is an asshole to stay. Yes, I know you can hug and make up but that's not the way the AQ works. What really happens is that people begin to associate various qualities with the assholes. They begin to see each other as bigger and bigger assholes. Consider the following statements:

- You are an asshole!
- You are a big asshole!
- You are a gigantic asshole!
- You are an enormous gaping asshole!
- You are without a doubt the greatest asshole I have seen!
- You are an asshole so incredibly ugly that you defy imagination!
- You are an asshole of such staggering stupidity and ugliness that it can only be matched by your personality!

Have you ever wanted to say any of the above to either your boss or some other little creep who has rubbed you the wrong way? Notice if you would, the strength of conviction in each of the statements. Notice also that certain qualities are being added increasing in size. Even if you can't say it, you can infer or think it! Remember Franklin in the marketing meeting when Slink Wirlwind did a "gotcha" on him? Guess what Franklin would have loved to say? What about the top guys that take a fall and get demoted to lower levels? Some actually stay there but can you imagine how they really feel about the guys who did it to them?

In the corporate culture, all the buzzards, hawks, owls, etc., get converted by each other slowly and methodically into assholes.

At this point in time the appearance changes in the eyes of the one who converted him. Suddenly the bird's posterior is showing through all of his fancy feathers. From now on the appearance gets worse and worse. Now let's look at our corporate tree. Each bird looks a little different as can be seen in the picture on the next page.

That's how it all starts - then at some peculiar point, all corporate qualities disappear and people just look like bigger and bigger assholes. If this could be visualized, you would probably imagine these people as small creatures with ever increasing posteriors, with big feet to hold them up, with small heads and beady eyes, and big snouts to slurp with. Disgusting isn't it?

Now Grunts, if you remember correctly, simply were useless citizens that lazed around in the mire with little direction or purpose - relatively harmless guys. But Slinks are a different group because they unfortunately retain power or influence and can be dangerous. They can trample you, drown you in trivia, turn others against you behind your back and do many devious things to you. Unlike the Grunt, their main purpose is to retain, by any means, their positions, regardless of their capabilities. Slinks are the most unproductive and dangerous species in the corporate culture. You may be able to think of a few who have "fallen from grace" but for some reason are still there. These guys have an agenda to get back up the tree and trample anyone in their way.

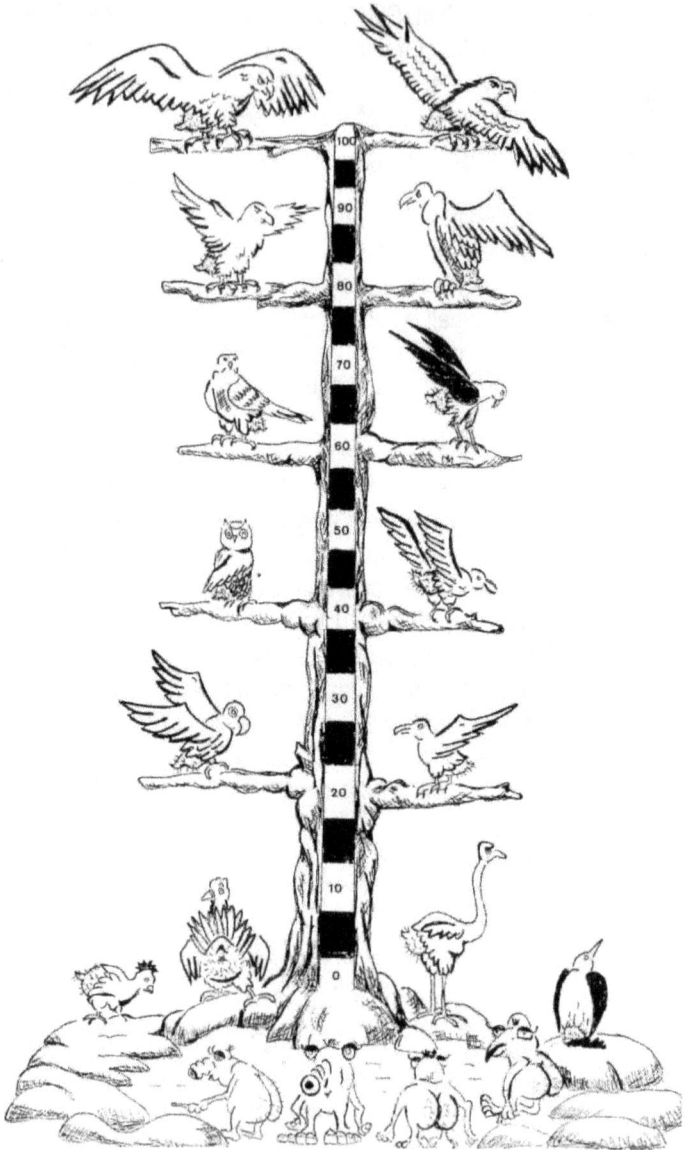

THE AQ EFFECT ON THE CORPORATE TREE

Obviously they have learned a few tricks in creating assholes and they would have picked up even more assholes on the way down. So the AQ is in total disequilibrium with their position. There is a name for these guys and they also have different characteristics but they can be grouped as **Slinks.**

THE CORPORATE SLINKS

STAGE 1   STAGE 2   STAGE 3

There are two types of evil Slinks - those who slurp (Slurper) and those who peck (Pecker). You have probably seen a slurper type quite often. He is the one who retains his position (above you) by slurping to someone with power.

His tactics, well developed, are used to constantly hide his incompetence, or to side with some powerful person who can protect him. The problem is that the incompetence is not usually hidden to those below. The Slurper just becomes one of the most disgusting creatures in the

THE SLURPER

company and is often quite obvious. This little insidious person just loves to blame others to protect or gain position. When these people gain power and authority they can be the most devious people around and they are difficult to dismantle in the corporate structure.

Now the other Slink – the Pecker – is an even more dangerous corporate creature. This one doesn't rely so much on defensive strategies like suckholing (the term used for someone who "sucks" up to others for personal gain). He is trained to use offensive tactics to peck others for survival.

He is the shifty creep who is always seen in your boss's office telling him things about which you cannot defend yourself, and that he can use to his advantage. Unfortunately they, again, have position and power and are totally incompetent.

THE PECKER

Enough said about the characters. This is a bit silly yes, but sometimes in many people, others just frustrate you they are so despicable and yet powerful. You just cannot understand why such creatures are allowed to thrive in a corporation. You can try to hide it but this does effect productivity and worst of all, your attitude.

In the next section we will finally examine where you and your AQ reside in this culture. It is now time to have a look at how to find out what your own AQ is and how you may fit into this new look at corporate structure.

7

SO HOW'S YOUR AQ TODAY?

Now we come to the business of determining your own AQ. The easiest way is to consider yourself as part of a physical group such as a Branch, Head office, Operation, Division, Plant, and so on. This is usually quite clearly indicated by a telephone list or better still, a list of employees and titles in your group. You, as a member of this group, are in one of three levels, mainly the executive, middle management or the working class. First, you must split the list into three groups and count the number of assholes within each group. In classifying assholes, follow the group guidelines below.

GROUP	EXAMPLE
Executive:	Chairman, Vice Chairman, Presidents, Managing Directors, Directors, Vice President, Assistant Vice President, or equivalent titles
Middle Management:	Superintendent, Manager, Treasurer, Controller, Foreman, Chief, Supervisor, or equivalent
Workers:	The rest

Assholes are:	Ones you have thought, inferred, called, told, treated in a negative way
	Ones you do not like
	Ones you have disagreed with
	Ones you have talked to others about as stupid
	Ones you consider useless, inferior, incompetent
	Ones you have had to reprimand
	Ones you have reminded of policies, procedures
	Ones you have taken advantage of
	Ones you have treated badly indirectly or directly
	Ones you have bullshitted or lied to
	Ones that you have taken things away from

The way it works seems to be that you must not be forgiving just because the guy was nice today, even after your fierce argument yesterday. This doesn't take him off your list! If you are high up the management ladder, it becomes more difficult to assess or enumerate those you have converted to assholes. This is because it may have been indirect. Remember Franklin Hardass when he sent a memo to all plant employees to cut coffee breaks by 3 minutes? Frank was treating everyone in the plant like assholes, regardless of what he thought he was doing. So you must think about all those situations where you gave somebody a bad review, had to remind someone about policies or when you sent nasty memos – regardless of reason or justification.

Let us use an example at Steadfast Meats and a list of all the employees. Let's look at Fred Fantasy's AQ at corporate

	EXECUTIVE	POSITION
A	Boomer Steadfast	Chairman of the Board
A	Franklin Hardass	President and CEO
	Scoot Blastoff	VP Operations
	Flash Spreadsheet	VP Finance & Administration
A	Slink Wirlwind	VP Planning
	Herbert Hoyle	VP Engineering
A	Angus Steadfast	VP Projects
	Murk Muddler	VP Legal & Corp. Affairs
	4 Assholes of	8 Total

headquarters. The corporate offices therefore constitute a physical group within which we will calculate various AQ's. It will be noticed that for the ease of explanation, the list has been split into the three levels. I need to tell you something about this list. In my own corporate travels, I encountered these particular characters so a name has been chosen to reflect that character and I have exaggerated them just a little bit! As you get to learn more about these people, you may even find close similarities to many in your own corporation. Now here is the Management Group.

	MANAGEMENT	POSITION
	Marcus Mule	Manager Projects
	Fred Fantasy	Manager Planning
A	Randolf Snooper	Director Personnel
	Clepto Superbyte	Dir. Inform Tech
	Micro Tabulate	Chief Accountant
A	Bill Blastoff	Ass. Man. Planning
	Donna Dingdong	Man. Marketing
	Grunt Hollowhead	Sup. Projects
A	Pomp Crotchley	Sup. Personnel
	Oscar Ostrich	Controller

A	Kevin Baloney	Sup. Ind. Relations
A	Prim Strutland	Sup. Admin. Services
A	Willy Liplock	Assist. Man. Operations
	Cut Thrasher	Sup. Systems & Oper.
	Gross Fartley	Man. Corporate Affairs
A	Barf Chapstick	Man. Legal
	Slime Mealymouth	Sup.Mech. Engineering
A	Horace LaPrick	Sup. Ranch Operations
	Clone Mimicker	Sup. Ind. Engineering
A	Switcho Stumpbrain	Manager Engineering
A	Wimp Wishwash	Sup. Support Services
	10 Assholes of	**21** Total

And finally, here are all the guys that do the work.

	WORKERS	POSITION
A	Gayle Grimley	Acc. Payables Clerk
	Moose Baxter	Special Serv. Coord.
A	Hump Pussywhip	Sr. Financial
A	Feelo Ballsack	Jr. Draftsman
	Buff Windbag	Sr. Financial Analyst
A	Cirilla Gorilla	Sr. Systems Analyst
	Sleeze Huffer	Sr. Engineer
	Quirk Multiples	Systems Analyst
	Fanny Bumwiggle	Secretary – Legal
A	Lardo Billobum	Solicitor
A	Irk Guffer	Accountant
A	Lila Memomangler	Legal Clerk
	Dork Assgrabber	Intermed. Draftsman
A	Sam LeSlam	Project Account
	Oink Freaker	Admi. Assistant
A	Slip Goofball	Special Proj. Eng.
	Jaybird Warpmatter	Engineer
	Lou Kabbagetop	Sr. Planning Advisor

	Name	Title
	Viola Broadbum	Int. Mech Engineer
	Bula Bugle	Business Analyst
	Spasmo Mover	Industrial Engineer
A	Korno Klutz	Engineer
	Vera Sparkle	Receptionist
	Dudley Dwarfbrain	Marketing Analyst
	Fats Gutstuffer	Computer Operator
	Birtha Bitchalot	Sr Filing Clerk
A	Jock Flasher	Supply Clerk
	Souse Growler	Int. Mech. Engineer
	Tina Tinkle	Operator
	Polly Perfect	Personnel Assistant
A	Wormley Crawler	Jr. Engineer
	Slim Twinkle	Designer
A	Bang Loudmouth	Systems Analyst
	Karen Klutz	Secretary – Eng.
	Dink Primrose	Sr. Accountant
A	Moira Mouthpeice	Executive Secretary
	Flirt Shameless	Coord. Office Ser.
	Wendy Worker	Filing Clerk
	Olga Titwhopper	Executive Secretary
	Buzz Bottle	Int. Planner
	Calc Theorem	Marketing Engineer
A	Marf Garfle	Accounting Clerk
	Grog Stinky	Engineer – Planning
A	Harvey Hotshit	Planner
A	Barry Brass	Int. Engineer
	Blam Featherflash	Marketing Analyst
	Warp Monkeynuts	Programmer
	Milo Muff	Support Person
	Suzy Bubbles	Accounting Secretary
A	Dork McPork	Coordi. Ranching
	Perky Shortwhip	Sr. Advisor
A	Bark Banana	Legal Assistant

A	Wino Dingbat	Business Analyst
A	Rolly Growl	Budget Coordinator
	Nose Grindstone	Jr Designer
	Crass Farkle	Project Engineer
A	Moon Flasher	Engineer – Design
	Milly De Dilly	Secretary
	Brenda Breeder	Personnel Clerk
	Piles Bumrubber	Designer
A	Herf Honker	Solicitor
	Ruff Honker	Jr. Programmer
	Garfle Greymatter	Systems R&D
A	Whipply Grizzlepuss	Draftsman
A	Sac Meddler	Personnel Clerk
A	Grim Rectum	Planner
A	Jerk Jerkins	Eng. – Mechanical
	Tina Droop	Executive Secretary
A	Marcus Mule	Financial Analyst
	Rhonda Grinder	Secretary
	Eric von Shithead	Industrial Rel. Clerk
	28 Assholes of	**71** Total

First, you must place an **A** beside each one on the list whom you classify as an asshole (as per the previous guidelines at the start of the chapter). You may have already noticed that I have marked some... this is Fred Fantasy's AQ calculation. You need to do this for each group and find how many assholes you marked out of the total for the group. For example, Fred thinks that 4 of the 8 executives are assholes. When Fred goes through the management list, he marks down 10 of the 21 Management people. Then when he goes through the worker list, he comes up with 28 assholes in a group of 71. Now he can take these numbers and place them on a summary tabulation to calculate the percentage of assholes. Fred has a BASIC AQ of 42% (total assholes/total employees).

GROUP or LEVEL	NUMBER ASSHOLES	GROUP TOTAL
Executive	4	8
Middle Management	10	21
Workers	28	71
TOTALS	42	100
	BASIC AQ	42%

Now this BASIC AQ in its simple form is a pretty good indication of your AQ level, particularly if the company is small. The trouble is that you may work for a huge corporation and therefore your AQ may appear insignificant overall, yet the local AQ or the group that you work with may reflect a high AQ. Obviously, the local AQ is more relevant so you need to use the people in the corporation that are local to you. As you gain a higher status in the company, there is a need to expand your list, but normally, the physical location of the groups dictates. The other aspect is that there are certain key modifiers of the AQ. For this reason, you can use the more technical method to modify your Basic AQ. Here is how you do this.

You must weight each group by a ratio. This means looking at each group individually and calculating your RAW AQ for each group. Then you multiply each RAW AQ by a predetermined weight (taken from the AQ METER). The total of the result will be your "RAW AQ". Go through each group and calculate Raw AQ.

GROUP or LEVEL	NUMBER ASSHOLES	GROUP TOTAL	PERCENT ASSHOLES	WEIGHT	RAW AQ
Executive	4	8	50	x .20	10
Middle Man.	10	21	48	x .40	19
Workers	28	71	39	x .40	16

The next procedure involves modifying the Raw AQ depending upon how many of your *line supervisors* are on your AQ list. The reason for modifying the AQ in this manner is to consider the impact your immediate bosses can play if anyone of them are on your list. Needless to say, if you<u>r</u> boss is on your AQ list, then you could be on shaky ground. If <u>his</u> boss is also on the list then you may be on dangerous ground. If the <u>next</u> boss is also on your list then you may indeed be living in a very precarious corporate world... unless your position is such that you are able to displace one of these guys. In order to bring your position back into line with your AQ, you should be contemplating moving out before they send you down one of the productivity slides. It should go without saying that your most immediate supervisors are the ones who can most affect your corporate growth and attitude. Your immediate boss, therefore, will damage you or your AQ the most. For this reason we must compute the AQ

YOUR BOSS	**.25**	*.25*
HIS BOSS	**.15**	*.15*
NEXT BOSS UP	**.10**	*.10*
TOTAL MODIFIER		*.50*

modifier by giving less weight to the asshole boss who is further away. This we call the "LINE AQ". For example, let's look at Fred again. Fred is the Manager of Planning and has his boss Slink Wirlwind ticked off, plus Slink's boss Franklin <u>and</u> the Chairman Boomer! So here is how Fred would modify his Raw AQ.

Fred must tick off which of the three supervisors up his supervisory line are on his list. He therefore ticks off all three modifiers in the little table, adds these up and gets a total of .50 as the modifier as you can see on the right. If Fred had only his

78

immediate boss classified as an asshole he would only have .25 as the modifier.

Now we must multiply this number times the "LEFTOVER AQ". Leftover AQ is simply 100 less your Raw AQ as calculated previously. Finally, there is one more step to get to your real AQ.

Your real AQ is the total of your Raw AQ plus the Modifier times the Left Over AQ. Note that the

TOTAL POSSIBLE AQ	100
less RAW AQ	45
EQUALS LEFTOVER AQ	55

Modifier times the Left Over AQ is the "Line AQ". Thus your real AQ, is the total of your RAW AQ and your LINE AQ.

In Fred's case he would get 72. He would add a whopping 27 points to his RAW AQ of 45 because he has all three line

LEFTOVER AQ	times	**MODIFIER**	equals	**LINE AQ**
55	X	.5	=	27
		PLUS RAW AQ		45
		EQUALS YOUR AQ		72

supervisors on his list. Now just think about that for a minute. If you thought all of your line supervisors were assholes, would you not think that you were on dangerous ground?

Now that we know how to calculate an AQ, let us examine its relation to the AQ Meter. Once you have determined your AQ, you can then look at where you are on the meter. The next page shows the AQ Meter with the related positions. It also shows you how to calculate your AQ on the same sheet... shouldn't you have one of these pasted on the wall of your office?

For example, if your AQ is 42, then you should be at a supervisory level. If you are just at a junior position, with an AQ of 42, then you are in AQ-DISEQUILIBRIUM. If you are in such a situation then this is a signal that you may be in trouble. If, on the other hand, your AQ is lower than your position warrants, this is ok but you may not be able to progress beyond a certain point in the climb upwards. If you have the AQ Virus, this means that at some point you may have to treat people like assholes and this may go against your nature - the reason an AQ may be too low.

Let's get back to Fred Fantasy. Fred ended up with an AQ of 72. On the AQ Meter, this means that Fred should be ready for a Director position. This is not so good for Fred as he is still a manager so he is in AQ Disequilibrium. The fact that he has his line supervisors on his AQ list is good, but according to AQ'ISM he needs to start thinking about telling people they are assholes directly. As a manager, he can only call people assholes. He wants to take this opportunity with a few people to assert himself so he can impress those line supervisors and get promoted.

THE AQ METER: HOW'S YOUR AQ TODAY?

Scale	Prefix	Title	Zone
100	ARE	Chairman	UPPER ECHELON
		President	
90		Executive Vice President	
		Vice President	
80	TREAT	Treasurer	
		General Manager	
70		Controller	
		Division Manager	TRAMPLE and GROPE
60	TELL	Director	
		Manager	
50		Asst Manager	
		Chief	
40	CALL	Supervisor	
		Coordinator	
30		Senior	
		Representative	LOWER REACHES
20	INFER	Intermediate	
		No Prefix on Title	
10		Junior	
		Trainee	
0	THINK	Zero	

	DATE OF SURVEY	

GROUP OR LEVEL	ASSHOLES	TOTAL	RATIO	WEIGHT	AQ
EXECUTIVE				x 20	
MIDDLE MANAGEMENT				x 40	
WORKERS				x 40	
				TOTAL RAW AQ	

LINE MANAGEMENT	✓	MOD	AMT
IMMEDIATE SUPERVISOR		.25	
NEXT LINE SUPERVISOR		.15	100
3RD LINE SUPERVISOR		.10	
TOTAL MODIFIER		X	=	LINE AQ

LINE AQ	+	RAW AQ	=	CURRENT AQ

CALCULATING YOUR AQ

Ok, we now know how to calculate an AQ. But what does it mean? Well, let us take four good AQ Virus examples from Steadfast Meats and get to meet some characters plus get a look at their AQ's. We will examine the AQ meter in detail and see how this can apply to us. Are you ready for this? These are real characters that I have worked with; names changed to suit the innocent!

CASE 1: SCOOTER BLASTOFF

Scooter is the Vice President of Operations. He is part of the Upper Echelon. In his quest upwards, Scooter has had to learn how to tell many people that they are assholes. This was hardly difficult for Scoot because he was a pretty big one himself... although he never thought so. Much of this he has accomplished by using his favorite expression that he is becoming *"disappointed in the performance."* The fact is that Scooter delegates things so fast in such a deluge that it is difficult for anyone to maintain consistent performance. Just recently, Scooter learned that it was much more effective to treat people as assholes directly - *"be direct,"* he says, *"pressure shakes the loose turds out of the sack pretty fast – it's the sticky ones you want anyways - who wants to waste time motivating dumb bunnies and assholes?"* It was this attitude that allowed Scooter to move into the executive, simply because he ceased to look like and be *"one of the boys"*.

If we look at Scooter's RAW AQ, we find that it is fairly high (75). This is because, as pointed out, Scooter shows less and less tolerance for slackers and low producers. *"They wouldn't get away with that kind of shit if they worked for me!"* he would say. Now Scooter reports to Franklin Hardass and his next line manager above Franklin is Boomer Steadfast, the owner and chairman. *"Boomer,"* he says, *"is just a senile old fart and Hardass is the biggest asshole in the company*!" This means that Scooter's LINE AQ is 10. (Modifier of .40 times LEFT OVER AQ of 25). The total AQ is 85, which seems high, but if we look at the AQ METER, we see that he is in AQ Equilibrium - situation normal.

In this case, the fact that Scooter has both of his line management on his AQ list is even ok. This is because he has already learned how to treat people as assholes and because his disagreement with his boss gives him the motive necessary to attempt displacing him. But let us suppose that Scooter was only an Operations Manager (i.e. one step down) with the same AQ of 85. Our meter shows that he is allowed 75 and obviously he would be in AQ Disequilibrium. In fact, he may even have three line supervisors so his AQ could be higher. In this case, his position would not support an AQ of 85, and with his bosses on his list, he could well be on precarious ground. But why would Scooter be in AQ Disequilibrium? He may not have been deemed as executive material. He may not have learned to treat people as assholes for the good of the company. He may have been too obvious about his feelings to his superiors. And so on. In any case, the danger signals would be obvious.

CASE 2: OSCAR OSTRICH

Oscar is the Controller so he belongs to the middle management group. Very much unlike Scooter, Oscar is quiet and seemingly cool. The fact of the matter is that Oscar really doesn't like conflicts and he certainly doesn't like to discipline anyone. So Oscar tries to avoid conflicts, ignores chaos, and spends a lot of time either doing the work himself, keeping his head buried in the sand (numbers), or quietly grumbling in his office. Being quite sensitive, Oscar has, over a few short years, devastated his AQ. He has just kept adding to his list by thinking that others were assholes. Just recently, because of these boiling frustrations, he has begun to infer and call others assholes - but never directly.

So when we add up Oscar's AQ, we find it sits at 60. We also find that Oscar's boss, Scab Dancer is on the list as is Franklin Hardass who is Scab Dancer's boss. Boomer Steadfast, who is the 3rd line supervisor is not on Oscar's list yet because he has not had much to do with him. Oscar doesn't like his boss much because he is "*two-faced*" and "*makes stupid irrational decisions*". "*Franklin Hardass*," he says, "*just never seems to listen*". This brings Oscar's AQ up to 76, well above what his position can support, so Oscar is in AQ-Disequilibrium.

Oscar is currently caught in a terrible dilemma - he doesn't particularly want to call people assholes and he certainly doesn't like to tell people they are assholes, and far be it to actually treat them like assholes. But his boss keeps telling him: "*Oscar, you can't go anywhere without moxy.*" Oscar's productivity is also suffering since he spends more and more time mumbling to himself - adding assholes to his list. It is just a question of time before Oscar takes a trip down a productivity slide if something isn't done. So far, Oscar's boss tolerates the situation because Oscar is a competent accountant and a nice guy, but as Scab puts it: "*I am getting tired of solving some of your problems, Oscar - we are not pleased with your performance*".

CASE 3: ERIC VON SHITHEAD

Eric is in the working class, working as an Industrial Relations Clerk. Eric reports to Kevin Balony who then reports to Scab Dancer. Eric's greatest problem is that he is simply not a very nice human. His personality, like a torn boot, is ragged and dirty. He would be classed as a Super Slurper, hardly adding to his credibility. Eric keeps his job by making sure that he takes care of his boss's every whim, and everyone knows it.

Eric just doesn't get along with too many people since he believes he is the smartest guy around and just can't wait to tell everybody - regardless of where and when - how important industrial relations is to the company. Nobody likes to listen to Eric anymore and some even tell him to "*piss off and bother someone else*". Others can be seen accelerating their walks by his office to avoid him seeing them. It is hard for Eric to understand this since he thinks he is so smart and company conscious.

Within a very short three years, Eric has tallied up a fairly impressive AQ. While various superiors have even told Eric to "*cool it*", others have told him to "*piss off*". Others try to ignore him - without attempting to hide their actions - the end result is to lift Eric's AQ. With a RAW AQ of 50 and the two line superiors above his boss on the list, Eric has a total AQ of 63. Now this may not seem like much, but Eric is only allowed an AQ of around 20 - very dangerous indeed - particularly at such a junior level. Eric has certainly learned how to *tell* and *call* but his position does not allow him these luxuries - remember the jumping of AQ Phases? No, no, no... it just can't be done. So Eric is also in Disequilibrium. Worst of all, he hasn't used the phases of infer, tell, call, etc. in step with his rising AQ to attain the equivalent position.

In fact, only Eric's boss, Kevin Balony is willing to stand up for him. This saves Eric from being fired since Kevin insists that Eric does good work and is a devoted company man. The fact is that Kevin likes to have the creep catering to him. The situation, however, is quite precarious in that the day Eric gets on Kevin's AQ list could indeed be the day a change rapidly occurs.

CASE 4: DONNA DINGDONG

Donna is the Manager of Marketing, residing in the Middle Management Class. Donna reports to Slink Wirlwind who reports to Franklin Hardass. Donna, quite clearly, is just a happy worker as she flits about dreaming up projects. Donna has only been there a year, having been hired by Slink for her credentials. Donna was a Professor of Economics, with virtually no practical experience. So Donna has had little time to develop her AQ. She has only had a few bad experiences, mostly chauvinistic encounters, so her RAW AQ sits at about 10. Franklin Hardass, the president, however, has made her list, so her line AQ adds another 14 points. Her total AQ of 24 is still well below what her position allows (mainly 55) as a department manager.

Being lower than the allowed equilibrium AQ is not yet a problem with Donna . It will become a problem, however, if she is required to utilize the AQ Phases which support that position, or she raises her AQ above that allowed for her position. What will happen is that she will not be able to come across as aggressive, put people in their place, threaten them, or change rules. This will do the opposite of Oscar and Eric, and allow others to take advantage of her. The AQ disequilibrium will work against her because she is just wrapped up in a nice little world, not paying attention to those clods and sods who are paying attention to their AQ's.

We now come to see the delicate balance between one's AQ, one's position and how those with the AQ Virus create corporate assholes. We have studied the AQ and we have seen what it means. We have also seen how to monitor it as a measure of one's corporate progress and cultural health. Next, we will look more closely at some corporate characters and their main avenue of direct communication - the meeting. We will see the AQ in Action.

8

WHY NOT HAVE A MEETING?

Up until now, we have talked about the concepts of AQ'ISM, how it relates to individual corporate members, and how the AQ-METER is able to quantify one's status within the company. We also had brief encounters with some of the corporate members and traveled with Franklin Hardass as he climbed to the Presidency. As we began to apply the theories, we had brief encounters with some of the other members of Steadfast Meat Packers Ltd. Now it is time to further study the players within the company and we will also examine the main communication and information exchange mechanism - the meeting.

THE BUSINESS OF MEETINGS

The corporate meeting is an extremely interesting mechanism. It is one of the most convenient ways of assembling, disseminating, exchanging and evaluating information quickly - at least in principle. Meetings, it seems, like our corporate citizens, become more and more regimented and predictable as we move higher up the corporate pyramid. Indeed, if handled properly, meetings can be effective ways of conducting corporate business. And yet it is the one mechanism that most everyone has to learn from scratch and by experience. For example, the power of meetings and the power of writing corporate "memos" cannot be under emphasized as necessary instruments to corporate growth. It is odd that these are not taught in school - the exception possibly being a Business College. Most professionals must learn to write and how to conduct themselves at meetings on their own initiative - before they can rise.

Meetings are the place where each can assess (and undress!) the other - it is the place where *"men are made or destroyed"*. It is here that everyone is at the same elevation as opposed to sitting in the tree at his or her relative statures. Here they can look good or foolish depending upon how they have learned the meeting/memo game. This becomes more and more important as one moves higher up the ladder. In fact one's professional ability in the area of original training (i.e. Engineering, Science, etc.) becomes less and less important. The training or degree just becomes a paper credential with little depth to it. Executives will always tell you that:

1. They do not have time for details since that is what the support staff is hired to take care of...
2. The bottom line and the cost benefit analyses are the key factors...
3. They have a long list of technical and management experience...
4. They are not yet convinced of the merit of your proposal.

There are four main reasons for this attitude. First, they usually remember very little about their training because they either forgot it or it is outdated. Secondly, corporations are essentially financial animals and they must be able to think and behave in financial dogma. Thirdly, they spend so much time in meetings, listening to problems and proposals, that they have no time for anything else. Fourthly, meetings are a good way of avoiding a formal commitment – i.e. discuss it instead and see what the others think first. Well, of course this may be a cop-out to hide their lack of knowledge, but on the other hand, they have picked up a new knowledge, which the technologists have yet to learn - Meeting Technology! This knowledge must be gained with the rise in AQ.

And so we have the business of meetings - the business to which this section is devoted. We will first investigate certain prototype meetings and then look at the players within each meeting. From these meetings we will attempt to develop some conclusions.

MEETINGS–THE MEDIUM OF PROGRESS?

Before I identified three levels as typically represented by the executive, the middle management and the workers. These three groups, I said, represent the corporate functions of Decision Making, Doing and Working. Although each group holds meetings that have the fundamental purpose of exchanging information quickly, we find that the individual style, format and content differ within each group. The working class has a tendency to provide, gather and process information. Middle management (the Doers) have meetings to coordinate, analyze and report information. And at the top, the executives (Decisions Makers) have meetings to direct, evaluate and decide upon information. So we have three types of meetings:

STAFF OR DEPARTMENTAL (Workers) This includes the working force, relating to individual isolated groups, departments or functions. These meetings are oriented towards providing, gathering and processing information.

PROJECT OR INTERDEPARTMENTAL (Middle) This includes middle management people who attempt to organize, analyze and report information on sub-projects or functions for which they are responsible. They consolidate and report progress, findings, etc. in accordance with some executive guidelines.

COMMITTEE OR EXECUTIVE (Upper) These meetings are made up of senior management and executive members who review and evaluate the information or results provided to them. Their function is to make decisions on this information - having the power to reject or accept proposals.

It should be noted that there are two sides to each meeting. That is, although the executives can decide upon the results presented, they must also be able to present, direct or execute the procedures necessary to get the results. While middle management meetings are to provide, analyze and consolidate information, the participants must be able to supervise, manage and present the activities that will provide the results. Finally, worker meetings that are to provide the basic information, must also have the mechanism to present it. So the presentation and the evaluation of the information are the key ingredients to any meeting.

It is in this aspect that meetings bare their prime purposes, for they show everyone who matters how any individual can handle both presentation and evaluation aspects to the "good of the company". That is, how does he evaluate, manage or do what he is responsible for? In any company, therefore, it is wise to pay attention to this aspect. Thus we have the LAWS OF PROGRESS:

LAW 1: You will progress only when you "do your job well".

LAW 2: Your "job competency" will be judged by someone above you.

LAW 3: You must "convince" someone above you that you are doing well.

Well, if you dare to venture into this arena, the meeting is the quickest way to progress. This is where you can "show off" to those above you. This is called exposure.

You can show that you do your job well and you can convince others besides your boss that you have great potential. On the other hand, it could be a quick way of proving to those above you that you are a real twit.

Meetings, it seems, always have "judges" in attendance. They will attempt to evaluate presentations and performance. Since the meeting's function is to deal with information, it will also be judged. The quick way to stardom is to get these judges together and put on a performance. A couple of good performances can even put pressure to bear on your own boss - if you so desire.

It should be noted that certain items in the LAWS OF PROGRESS are in quotes. These deal with your "competency" and the act of "convincing" someone of your competency. When one considers that, according to the PETER PRINCIPLE, each has a tendency to rise to his own level of incompetence, it makes a mockery of the competence judging process. Secondly, how one convinces these incompetent people is also quite a joke, particularly if one tries to relate this to his technical ability. In conjunction with the LAWS OF AQ'ISM, we find that because corporate people constantly seek profit, power and prestige, meetings become great gatherings of corporate assholes that meet to "jockey" for position. Everyone attempts to impress someone else, regardless of whether someone else is an asshole. And, because companies exist to produce and make profits, it follows that the best way of impressing superiors is to convince them that you can get things done in a better or more efficient way - convince them that you can affect the bottom line of time and money. When you consider that the three types of meetings provided, analyzed, then evaluated information successively, and each group became less concerned with details because they were closer to their levels of incompetence, you begin to seriously question how companies survive. But this is the game you must play. Let us sum up with a new AQ law:

MEETINGS BRING TOGETHER A GROUP OF INCOMPETENT ASSHOLES WHO ATTEMPT TO EXCHANGE AND PRESENT EVER-DETERIORATING INFORMATION IN SUCH A WAY AS TO IMPRESS EACH OTHER SO THEY CAN BECOME BIGGER ASSHOLES AND AFFECT COMPANY PROFITS.

Sounds quite horrible doesn't it? It is so because most of these players have a dose of AQ Virus. Of course it need not be so but if one could sit outside meetings and watch the proceedings, he would indeed see quite a show, particularly at higher levels where AQ's are fairly high. Think about the number of corporate failures every year. Do you think this asshole phenomenon has anything to do with it? The funniest meetings are where INTER-ASSHOLISM has taken its toll and ASSHOLE SATURATION is evident, particularly if any SLINKS are present. Let us examine meetings with the AQ Virus well entrenched in more detail.

In the next section we will attempt to examine corporate meetings from an AQ light. We know there are three important types, corresponding to the three AQ Levels. We will attempt to show how the AQ phenomenon is at work in these meetings and identify critical behaviors that we will use in the following chapters on AQ tools.

To do the examination, we must look closer at Steadfast Meats, its corporate members and their meeting. We must look at the flow of information as it proceeds upwards into the echelon from the lower reaches - through the meeting. First, let us look at Steadfast Meats.

STEADFAST MEAT PACKERS LTD. A GENERAL PROFILE

STEADFAST MEATS is what one would consider a medium sized company. It currently has annual revenue of $50 million. Beginning in the early 1950's, the company struggled along with one ranching operation and one plant near Queersteer, Alberta until the mid 1960's when commodity prices and the economy began to inflate rapidly. The company was originally founded in 1952 by the Steadfast brothers who began by expanding from a ranching operation. As such, the company is privately owned by old Boomer P. Steadfast who retains the position of Chairman of the Board. Boomer, almost single handedly built the company despite his brother Prickley Steadfast who was committed to an institution shortly after the first plant was built. Through some fairly slick transactions in the 60's, Boomer acquired some excellent ranches and started construction on two more plants, one in Ontario and one in Manitoba, both with small ranching operations.

It was this fluke of foresight that allowed the company to take full advantage of the major bull market in meat prices. In this respect, the company profited quite handsomely through the late 1960's and early 1970's, thus allowing various side ventures to take place and head office overhead to build dramatically.

Through the 1970's the company expanded its head office from 20 to its current status of 100 people. Being flush with profit and many new ideas, there was always money available to build a new corporate head office, purchase jets, buy new plant equipment, build luxurious offices, set up research projects and attempt various diversifications. This diversification scheme resulted in a small plant and ranch being purchased in the Outback of Australia, with a small corporate office in Sydney.

Just recently, there has been a move towards operations in Columbia and South Africa. The Australian venture has never seen any profit and in fact, it cost more to set up the "controlling office" and move some of the old deadbeats from head office than it did to buy the operation. Actually, although most of the executives have been to the plush Sydney office, none have had the courage to travel for days through the Outback to see the plant operation.

So old Boomer, now 75 years of age, is deemed as completely senile by the executives, but he is the controlling shareholder so there is nothing anyone can do to get rid of him. It seems that Boomer mutters constantly about overhead and stupid diversifications at the board meetings. The executives have learned how to gang up on old Boomer and keep him from pointing his cane to fire someone. Actually, Boomer's two greatest problems are how to spend all his money and how to keep his pants from continuously creeping up the crack of his bum. The whole company has an image of Boomer P. Steadfast - he is the old Growler typically seen hovering over his cane, growling at his $500.00 shoes, frantically picking at the back of his pants, trying to extract the material that is constantly being ingested by his anatomy.

Boomer would love to fire those who giggle and scoff at him but he couldn't remember their faces. *"Ungrateful roaches"* he mumbles to himself as he picks away at his pants.

Franklin P. Hardass is currently the President and Chief Executive Officer of the company. We have already met Frank. Years back Boomer took a shine to Franklin because *"Franky has moxy"* as he put it. Franklin worked his way up from the slaughtering section of one of the plants over some twenty years. Franklin now resides at a plush head office that contains 100 people. The head office structure is fairly typical with a pyramid hierarchy of 8 Executives at the top of the areas called Operations, Finance & Administration, Planning, Marketing, Engineering, Projects and Legal & Corporate Affairs. Below this, 21 Middle Management types control some 71 white-collar types covering various support and head office functions. I am sure you can picture the typical structure.

This structure represents a fair overhead strain on the operations since each plant must pay a "management fee" to support the head office. And, as mentioned, the near decade of prosperity allowed various services to expand into fairly extravagant areas.

Each operation typically has a plant manager who reports directly to the Vice President of Operations at head office. Plant managers take responsibility for various plant areas depending upon the size of the operation. This could involve Ranching, Slaughtering, Butchering, Processing, Packing, Distribution and Administrative Services. Administrative Services usually includes the functions of Accounting, Sales, Engineering and Office Services.

Where possible, administrative services have been kept to a minimum since support comes from head office. Needless to say, the Administrative and Technical Services are separate sections of the plants, with fairly plush offices. The exception to this structure is the new Australian office that reports to the President directly - through the Sydney office.

So here we have a fairly successful, medium sized company that has had some time to let the AQ phenomenon take hold. Some fairly major projects have been initiated through prosperous times and these have caused some substantial liabilities in terms of outstanding loans and deferred taxes. With the current economic and price reversals occurring, the company has become sensitive to the high overhead and increasing liabilities. Over the last three years, therefore, various pet projects have been cut and an emphasis on increased productivity is evident.

Because things have been fairly rosy, people have been allowed to "do their own thing" almost without question. Staff turnover has been minimal and therefore AQ's have all had a chance to mature to great heights - asshole saturation is evident. Now more than ever, the executives are looking for new opportunities to generate cash flow and to sustain their level of corporate/personal living standards. To make matters worse, there are rumors that Boomer Steadfast is hiring efficiency consultants from New York to scrutinize the activities of the company.

So everyone is trying to keep their little empires, liberties and freedoms intact, looking for every opportunity to either put the empire to work, look busy or justify its existence. You will quickly realize that this is actually very much like many other companies.

THE MEETING AGENDA

We have discussed the business of meetings. If there is any credibility to our AQ Laws, then it has become pretty obvious that these meetings bring together a group of incompetent assholes who attempt to exchange and present ever-deteriorating information in such a way as to impress each other so that they can become bigger assholes and affect company profits. Steadfast Meats, with its history and structure, certainly helps to convince one of this, but let us closely examine meetings within Steadfast Meats.

It was mentioned that there are essentially three important meeting types, corresponding to the three corporate levels. Although these meetings provide the media for information exchange, they also provide the means for performance assessment. As we climb higher up the corporate structure, we find that meetings become more frequent and are more "organized". In the lower reaches, people have not yet learned to hold or conduct meetings, let alone control one. This is learned in the climb upwards. Worker meetings are therefore of a different nature than those of the upper two levels.

Quite often, there is a tendency to select key people from a lower status or group and "cast them to the wolves", so to speak. Thus, the "lower downs" have a chance to perform in front of the "higher ups" to have their cases presented and their performances judged. In certain cases, a "lower down" (usually in middle management) is presenting a new idea or recommendation. In other cases, a "lower down" may have been asked to be present as technical backup to a "higher up's" presentation. Clearly, this may also be the case with a middle management level meeting. Remember Franklin Hardass's experiences? Thus we have two levels of meetings where members can watch, learn, develop and try their hands at meeting techniques.

Every meeting will usually include key selected players and an agenda if it is reasonably organized. The key people are chosen so as to make relevant contributions or assessments and an agenda is set so as to prepare participants and minimize the time required to accomplish agenda objectives. As we go lower down the corporate levels, we find that these two ingredients become more and more "ad hoc" and disorganized. At the worst end, meetings can become shouting matches just to see who is the loudest - with no agenda, objectives or control. But, again, at the top, we find that meetings are controlled by one person who ensures that agendas are followed and that participants "keep on track". This is what one must learn if lofty positions are the objective.

Within STEADFAST MEATS, there are three issues that require approval at the executive level. In all three situations, various people have been involved in providing or creating reports with recommendations for approval. The three issues are as follows:

1. A world wide computerized communications network.
2. A standardization of corporate washroom facilities.
3. A new operation in Columbia, South America.

These three issues stem from three separate areas of the company. In the case of proposal number one, Clepto Superbyte, the Director of Information Technology is determined to make a name for himself and also get away from his current boss. He has thus put together a proposal for a worldwide computerized network with the help of his staff. He has also had to call upon other middle management people and use external services to put a report together. Basically Clepto is looking to keep his staff occupied since they could be on the verge of being cut.

In the second, Gross Fartly, the Manager of Corporate Affairs, in conjunction with Brenda Breeder, a personnel clerk, have put together a report for Randolf Snooper, the Director of Personnel. It so happened that Gross and Brenda who developed a passion for each other at the oddest moments, had a habit of whipping into executive washrooms for the odd "hug and feel session". It was through this activity that they noticed and even inadvertently disclosed certain non-standard features between the executive and public facilities. Upon realizing their mistake, they went to their boss Randolf, inventing the "employee complaint" tactic to cover up their indiscriminant activities. It worked! Randolf decided that he could use this to his advantage by presenting cost saving solutions to management and at the same time show that he and his employees were dedicated. In addition, he could show that he was attempting to honestly address employee concerns before they got out of hand. This would create considerable recognition for him.

In the third, Angus Steadfast, VP of Projects and Slink Wirlwind, the VP of Marketing, have a joint proposal to open a new plant operation in Columbia. Angus is in need of a project, while Slink is looking to do better than his Australian venture and also trying to get a new controlling office either on the Indian Ocean or in the Caribbean. His hope is to create the equivalent of the plush Sydney office and become the chief over there where he could "*open up vast opportunities for the company*" as he puts it. Needless to say he could live in the lap of luxury away from head office! Angus, on the other hand, has a bone to pick anyway and wants to show his uncle Boomer that he should be in charge - that only he can get an international cash flow moving - not like Franklin Hardass who wasn't part of the family anyway.

So the above three issues are scheduled for executive presentation and approval.

THE EXECUTIVE MEETING

Executives hold meetings to get information to quickly make decisions. The executives of STEADFAST MEATS have three proposals upon which they must take action. This they will do by assimilating the information presented and making a decision. The president has called a meeting and the agenda has been circulated along with relevant reports, two weeks prior. Since the three items on the agenda cover most of the areas of the company, all executives have been told to attend. In addition we have two new participants, mainly Clepto Superbyte and Randolf Snooper. They will be presenting their material. Although they may not be aware of it, they may be aspiring new victims or they may be new entries to the executive flock - whatever the case may be. Our meeting participants are as follows:

Franklin Hardass	PRESIDENT
Angus Steadfast	VP PROJECTS
Scab Dancer	VP FINANCE
Murk Muddler	VP LEGAL
Flash Spreadsheet	VP PLANNING
Herbert Hoyle	VP ENGINEERING
Slink Wirlwind	VP MARKETING
Scooter Blastoff	VP OPERATIONS
Clepto Superbyte	DIR. INFORMATION TECHNOLOGY
Randolf Snooper	DIR. PERSONNEL

An interesting aspect of these lofty leaders is that they are all real people and real people have idiosyncrasies along with their capabilities. If you could take away their fancy clothes and slick mannerisms, see their funny little pleasures and habits, what would they really look like? Well, let us REALLY get to know some of these "lofty" people and some of their habits. Most of all let us see how AQ'ISM has influenced them.

9

LET'S MEET THE DECISION MAKERS

The meeting we talked about has 10 attendees. Now there is something that I want you to understand. This is a serious meeting within the upper crust of the company. Remember that their AQ's must be pretty high just to be allowed in this meeting. And it is this lofty position that so many people in companies fear or respect. These guys are usually looked upon as solid characters with solid competence. Some of them really are but in most cases this is a real joke, because when you really look at the individual characters and strip away their position or corporate veil, they are some of the funniest, silliest characters around, especially when those AQ's are up in the 80's. I have to say that these characters you are about to meet are not made up. I have known these guys and watched them perform. Now, I may have exaggerated a few things but nevertheless they are just like any other person. The names chosen reflect their habits and characteristics. After all, we are exposing the corporation aren't we? Ok, let us meet the players.

FRANKLIN P. HARDASS

Franklin, to anyone who may be fairly new to the company, would be an Eagle. Remember the corporate hierarchy and the birds in the tree? To others, Franklin's ass is showing. As Chief Executive Officer he is the one to be looked up to and also the one that VP's attempt to dethrone. We have already been exposed to Franklin's story back in the previous chapter so we will not belabor that segment of his growth upwards in the company. Franklin learned how to fly high and soar over his domain. He learned how to identify victims quickly and attack mercilessly, particularly when provoked. It is this aspect that raises fear in those below him and it is this ability that guarantees him his high position from which he can shit upon others with considerable impact. In his quest upwards, he learned how to run meetings and people. He learned not to understand the word "no" unless he said it. He learned how to bullshit people and how to shit on them. He realized that it was easier to control technologists than it was to control technology, so Franklin's tactic was to display a wall full of credentials. These he used to hide his incompetence.

Franklin became a member of the Institute of Boardroom Brawlers of America. He joined the Exclusive Executive Manipulators Club, and the National Groinkickers Association, each time getting an impressive and awesome looking certificate to litter his wall. He even had several copies of his diplomas scattered about. With a Masters degree in Business Administrivia from Hardvard College and a Bachelors degree in Mechanical Engineering (he said), no one ever questioned his technical abilities.

Franklin always worked hard at what he did, and as everyone in the company knew, he worked his way up - right from the bottom. Back in high school, Franklin was fascinated by mechanical devices. This led him to get a job as an oilier in the slaughtering section of the original Steadfast Plant. Here he would oil mechanical devices - including the newly installed mechanical castrator device. All through university, he looked forward to watching and taking care of these devices - but it was the mechanical castrator that allowed Franklin his first move. Franklin had noticed that the cutter would more often than not, cut and drop scrotums quite indiscriminately forcing the nut-bucket haulers to occasionally reach out prematurely to get trampled by the cattle. "*I wanted to improve my education so that I could improve that device,*" Franklin would say, "*there are too many injuries*". And improve it he did - by developing a mechanical device that retracted and turned perpendicular upon scrotal impact. He was eventually made supervisor over the oilers and nut-bucket haulers.

When Franklin graduated from mechanical engineering, he expanded quickly into new areas, always trying to improve things. With the tenacity of a bulldog, he would target specific objectives and hold on until he solved the problem. Moreover, he rapidly learned how to control people. Franklin made his way up to the position of Plant Manager by learning how to get the most out of people through fear. Secondly, he was always finding ways to improve mechanical devices.

As Plant Manager, Franklin had time to take various courses and gain diplomas. His turning point was when he was able to use some of the boardroom groinkicker tactics that he had learned. He finally made his play against Slink Wirlwind and came out looking very cool - that was when Boomer Steadfast took an interest in him. After that Franklin looked forward to meetings where he could use key questions or phrases that made him look cool, objective, sincere and company conscious. What Franklin liked was that he didn't need to know anything about technology or even details to make someone look foolish - he just had to ask the right questions - and in a position of power he could make the question more pointed.

So Frank moved up in the company almost mercilessly, gaining an ever-increasing ability to exercise and maintain control - regardless of what was to be controlled. Frank would always subdue an emotional meeting or attack anyone who would deviate. He would even expel those who were unprepared. It was so bad that VP's who were unprepared for Frank's meetings would call in sick as they pretty well knew what would happen.

Well, this is Franklin Hardass, the President and Chairman of the executive committee meetings. His meetings could be summed up in Franklin's favorite statement: "*I don't give a shit what you talk about as long as it is orderly, relevant and is company business*".

ANGUS P. STEADFAST

Angus is the Vice President of Project Development. Angus is the nephew of the owner, Boomer Steadfast, and he is also the son of Prickley J. Steadfast, co-founder of the company. In fact Angus's second name is Prickley - carrying on his father's name. Angus has become a Vulture and could quite easily become a Condor, always seeking prey. His constant striving for the top spot has taken its toll on him, particularly when he was beaten out by an outsider. In his position, he is responsible for the development of new projects as well as coordinating the design and construction of new plants. Unfortunately, however, for the last 10 years there have not been any new projects to develop. So Angus has had very little to do except work diligently on his AQ.

Angus has clearly learned to be a stubborn, unyielding and uncompromising asshole to others. Just about everyone knows him to be a Vulture bordering on corporate Pecker. Remember the corporate Slinks? Even the sight of this man would unnerve someone. He has a loud rasping type voice, a scrotum type balding head and beady piercing eyes. Angus has a crooked lip that he says he got at an international karate competition. Actually he got kicked in the head by a cow while working on his father's ranch as a teenager.

Angus has three major problems. One is that he used to be an excellent engineer and project manager, being involved in the early construction projects of the company. This does not sound bad in itself. The problem is that Angus spends most of his time telling everyone that he is unsurpassed in his field. Secondly, Angus is part of the founding Steadfast family and he does not let people forget this. Angus's third problem caused him to fall from grace with his uncle, as we will see later.

As mentioned, it was Prickley J. Steadfast, and Boomer Steadfast who together founded the company, expanding from a ranch operation into a plant expansion. The Steadfast family, living in Queersteer, Alberta, was a fairly well established family, with considerable holdings and wealth. Although the brothers were fairly close, Boomer was by far the more industrious and ambitious, taking over when his brother was committed to an institution. It all started when Prickley got accidentally locked up in the barn with one of the larger and friendlier sows. No one could ever understand why but when they found Prickley two days later he was never the same - nor was the sow! For days Prickley would head for the barn each morning, with various articles of clothing for the sow. It just got worse and worse until the day Prickley brought the pig into the house dressed in gumboots and his wife's evening dress. Everything would have been ignored except that Prickley's wife was holding a little social party with all the community hoity-toits. It didn't take long to commit poor Prickley after that.

Thus Boomer took over the ranch and merged it with his own holdings, keeping the family together. Boomer had also taken a shine to Angus who, at the time, was studying industrial engineering at McHotshit University. Angus worked for Boomer as a ranch hand. It was natural to expect that Angus would have a position in his uncle's plant and become involved in the construction of new plants. And so he did, doing a respectable job in setting up and coordinating several projects with Boomer. He even did one by himself. Eventually, Angus took over as Manager of Project Development. In fact, Angus progressed quite well except for his little problem.

Angus had a bad habit that used to enrage Boomer. Angus always assumed that there wasn't a woman alive that could resist him. He figured that given his unsurpassed abilities, together with his good looks and suave nature, hot female passion was just a natural reaction. So Angus would purposely leave his fly down about a third of the way and keep a crumpled sock in his shorts. This, he thought, would tease the women mercilessly. Angus would stroll through the secretarial pool very carefully flashing his blazer to expose his bulge to the women, leering at them through his crooked teeth. Of course the girls would smirk and giggle, just creating a further come-on for Angus. Unfortunately, Angus used to come to management meetings, having forgotten his trek through the pool. As a result when Boomer retired, it was difficult to consider Angus as President.

Boomer would just make Angus the Vice President of Project Development and leave it at that. Since there wasn't anything on the books for new projects, Angus could do the least harm in this position. But Angus just got uglier, more obnoxious, and more perverted. In fact, it was even said that if provoked enough Angus would sometimes make advances that bordered on serious legal issues. In addition, having been involved in the early growth of the company, and bearing the Steadfast name, it became more and more difficult for Angus to not let people know who he was and what he could do. Although he could never confront Franklin directly, he would tell others that he was the real choice for President. Angus could often be heard saying that "*he would devote his life to the company and shit on anyone in his way or devour any cripples on the way up*". So Angus's engineering and management abilities just slid further and further away even though he would never admit it. Recently he had taken a Tough Kookie course and he now belonged to the Brotherhood of Loudmouths, so there wasn't much that he couldn't handle. With an extremely high AQ of 95, the only reason that Angus was still around was because he had received a large chunk of shares in the company from his father.

SCAB DANCER

Scab is the Vice President of Finance and Administration. He is responsible for all financial matters in the company and has also acquired some other major responsibilities like Personnel, Office Services and Information Technology. Scab, like Angus, is a predatory Vulture. There is a vast difference between the two, however, in that Scab is extremely dangerous in matters of attacking crippled victims. The slightest flutter of a victim will always result in a direct frontal attack. What is even more noteworthy is that Scab is capable of reversing a frontal attack and escaping without so much as a ruffled feather should his victim show any sign of retaliation. Angus, on the other hand, was more of a bag of wind. Being a big vulture, Scab is also quite capable of shitting profuse amounts upon others whenever possible.

Now Scab's performances at meetings are always superb - he knows how to hover around, probing at victims to see how healthy they are. Being in Finance, he has learned that his main purpose in life is to say no - simply because it is always Finance that must say no! He knows that this immediately puts his opponents on the defensive and this way he can judge the opponents state of health. His favorite tactics at any sign of response are predictable. *"What are the cost benefits?"* or *"You have not yet convinced me"* or *"So what is the bottom line?"* and *"We don't really see the merit yet"* are common probes to subdue others.

And whenever one of these probes gets a shabby response, Scab immediately takes it upon himself to speak for other executives. *"How do you expect us to waste our time on such a sketchy proposal?"* or *"We think you should table this again when you are better prepared"* or *"We are not yet satisfied of the proposed rate of return"* are sure ways of disabling victims for the benefit of the company. Scab knows precisely when to back off, shut up and still look good. Worse of all, he is always so friendly and nice outside the boardroom. But everybody knows Scab for the two-faced hypocrite that he is - unfortunately no one can trap him.

Scab is a middle-aged executive who moved into a lofty position quite rapidly. His boardroom performances did this for him being mercilessly "in tune" with making money, and being ruthless in dealing with those not prepared. Being clean cut, with a beaming grin, he always looks presentable in his endless supply of three-piece pinstriped suits.

It was only about three years prior that Scab was hired into Steadfast Meats as Chief Accountant. At that time he would constantly tell his employees about his superior training at the Chartered Institute of Stuffy Beancounters. His superiors were always informed of his superb experience. *"I've always worked in the low marginal utility industries"* he would say, *"where survival depends upon the skill of financial control. I got most of my experience in the meat business."*

What Scab really meant was that he worked in a small glue company that made parking stickers for employee cars at two packing plants in Horflehuff, Ontario. Actually they never made the stickers, they just put the glue on the back. Somehow an old fart named Herb Snorkle had made a go of this glue operation, building it up into a four man company. Herb liked Scab the first time he saw him so he gave him a job counting glue brushes - inventory control Herb called it.

Here he worked through high school getting his first exposure to accounting (counting was actually more appropriate). After about a year Scab suggested that each of the two brushers should be allowed two brushes each and this would save Herb the cost of inventory control. Herb was so impressed that he gave Scab a full time job counting the stickers sold - Senior Accountant Herb called it. This is where Scab learned all of the names of the executives in the packing plants. Eventually old Herb packed it in - it seems he had been sniffing too much of the glue.

Scab had saved up some money so he went to university to eventually earn a degree in commerce. Through the five years at university he somehow got a job at an auditing firm carrying the partners' briefcases whenever they required it. They eventually took pity on Scab and gave him a title as an Assistant Auditor. This company was a fairly shabby outfit doing the odd audit for some of the plants in the area. Just about the time Scab was graduating, the partners sensed that their company was going bankrupt so they made Scab a partner to absorb liabilities. Fortunate for Scab there were only a few residual liabilities. It was here that Scab learned some harsh lessons.

When the job at Steadfast Meats came up, Scab was able to boast a fairly impressive resume for a young graduate. Not only this, he knew many of the names of executives at competing plants - a natural for the job of Chief Accountant. In this job he didn't stay long, for back at the institute he had taken special courses such as Superscabbing and Taxes, Dress to Kill, Accounting for the Mafia, Sidestepping to Fame and Choosing Your Corporate Victims. It was not long before he was showing STEADFAST MEATS how to write-off stuff they hadn't even purchased yet. He could defer taxes without mercy. His move to Vice President was therefore fairly quick when the previous Vice President was fired.

In his new job as V.P. Scab inherited other areas that he knew nothing about. This, he realized, mattered very little in a boardroom - there is where he could perform, regardless of the technical details. "*Everything*", he said, "*reduces down to profit or loss*".

Being a two faced person, with a lust for victims, Scab is viewed by others as a disgusting creature. Most are jealous of his rise to power and many would love to see him "fall from grace". Others are quite envious of the superb "dancing" abilities that he exhibits during tough times.

Recently, Scab has become fairly cocky in his quick promotions so he talks more, leaving an "audit trail" of ideas and commitments. This, of course, makes it more and more difficult for him to dance around opponents. Just within the last few months, he has trained his secretary Mila Meatseaker, to always intercept telephone calls and inform people of some extensive meetings that Scab has to go to. Even if you catch Scab in his office, he will always say with a smile "*I am just leaving to go to an important meeting. Catch you later*". It is definitely easy to put Scab on your AQ list because he is so obviously two faced -

while smiling and chatting with you he is seeking information to use against you. The stupidity of it all is that Scab thinks that he is such a nice, honest, hard working executive. Scab's AQ is quite high because he treats people as stupid assholes - thinking that they are not aware of it.

MURK D. MUDDLER

Murk is the Vice President of Legal & Corporate Affairs. There is no better way to describe him except as a fat Buzzard - more considerately known as a Vulture. He is a short fat piglet of a man with bushy black eyebrows, big hairs sticking out of his nose and cheeks like a fat gopher. He has more hair on his knuckles than most people have on their arms. Murk has a vast wardrobe of three-piece suits - the $500.00 variety. The problem is that a big fat, hairy belly commonly forces its way through both shirt and vest. The size of the belly button is indeed noteworthy, particularly obvious when it sags over Murk's wide belt buckle, designed as part girdle to keep his spine from caving forward.

Murk's main asset to the company is that he has an incredible ability to confuse legal documents and issues. This, in many cases in the past, has proven to be very useful in escaping from some bad contracts. Murk is like a trained German Shepherd dog, who just sits waiting to attack a victim upon any given signal. Usually Franklin activates Murk with a *"What do you think about this matter, Murk?"* At that instant Murk will attack with an incredible deluge of wheretofors, heretoupons and notwithstandingto's that the legal profession would be proud of. Most opponents simply back off or sign just to avoid the abuse or looking stupid.

Murk got his law degree from the famous Confusem Institute of Law, after getting his commerce degree at the Belligerent Business College. Here he majored in Shabby Business and

Business Unethics, graduating at the top of his class. This wasn't so surprising since Murk was so gross and repulsive as a student that no one would associate with him - so he studied a lot. At law school, he would dream up little legal expressions like "*where to for and here upon with*" with which he could riddle legal documents. By the time he graduated he was so good that he even confused the Dean of the institute. In fact on many an exam, Murk was given a high mark because it was impossible to decipher whether Murk's answers were wrong.

Coming from a long line of backward rural slobs, Murk and his family were probably the closest to "missing links" that was possible without being gorillas. Murk, it seems, muttered his first words when he was 10 years old. It was quite a shock to hear him say *"Gwampa pwick out"* while sitting on his Grandfather's lap. The old man, as usual, had forgotten to flip his member back into his pants. Nobody had noticed since Murk was sitting on it.

When Murk said this, he immediately recalled his experience the previous day when he had forgotten to zip his fly and a lawyer came up to him and said: *"Look Gramps, I am a lawyer and let me offer you some advice. Hobbling around here with your prick out is an obscenity violation so cool it!"* What was happening was that the old man in his senile wisdom was associating "prick" with "lawyer". *"Jeez",* he said to Grandmother, *"the kid sounds like a lawyer. He's going to be a lawyer!"* From then on the family saved every penny to put Murk through school. It was quite an occasion when he finished high school at 24. Indeed it wasn't surprising that Murk pushed onwards - his family kept supporting him and he had few friends to detract him.

It wasn't at all surprising to see him hang up his shingle in his hometown. The sad thing was that Murk was actually quite capable, but no one really liked his looks or his manners. By this time, however, Murk had made a friend. He and his new buddy would get their trench coats and flash in front of the female gorillas at the zoo. They giggled and chortled like a couple of kids when the gorillas went wild.

Well, although they were normally quite discrete, his buddy became more involved and he got caught on a Sunday afternoon at the zoo. This was Murk's first defense case and he performed well - getting his buddy off on a technicality. That's what the judge called it for lack of a better way of describing the confusion during the case. Murk's practice didn't move along too well - most of the time defending his family - so he moved and took a job defending bums and perverts at the law firm of Groin, Porno and Porno. This is where Murk got his best experience defending many cases successfully. As a matter of fact, Murk defended Sam Suckhole at the time Franklin Hardass was working at the plant. Sam got himself into a bit of a situation and needed some special legal help.

There was no saving Sam from his problems - too many witnesses, but Murk did such an honorable job that Frank remembered him later at head office. It seemed that there were many odd cases around the plants, so Murk was asked whether he wanted a permanent position as Legal Advisor at Steadfast Meats. Naturally, Murk leapt at the opportunity.

As Legal Advisor, Murk was at his best - confusing legal issues - always to the advantage of the company. As Murk gained success in his work, he gained confidence and became more and more gross. When he was eventually promoted to Vice President, he found that he could use repugnant words such as "fuck" or "puke" and inject them into his legal jargon for an even more effective reaction. Or he could inject gross jokes into a discussion further distracting an opponent. Murk would love to stand up at a meeting and say things like "*Notwithstanding the heretofor of the fucking undertaking, what insofar of the goddam statements is the puke's allegations?"* He even learned that he could fart at a meeting and get away with it, except when Franklin was there. Having a short fat ass with cheeks of considerable depth, he could let a fart start rumbling out slowly, to let everyone raise their eyebrows before the final resounding thunder was unleashed. And the best part was the smell - this could really knock his opponents off guard.

Well, not many executives think too much of Murk, and the middle management group is bewildered as to how Murk keeps his job when Franklin is so strict. But even Franklin has warned Murk about his habits. To the rest, Murk is so gross that he is funny. Murk's AQ is high because he likes to call people "useless pukes" or "stupid assholes" whenever he gets a chance - particularly at company social meetings where he can drink freely.

FLASH E. SPREADSHEET

Flash is the Vice President of Planning - a position that was created where he could do the least harm. The last thing that Steadfast Meats needed was a plan - they knew where they were going - more profits! Flash is a Vulture, having lived upon the spoils of life. The strange thing is that he is a lucky Vulture in that he somehow always manages to come out of the weirdest situations smelling like a rose. His biggest problem is that he is subject to panic - this making him well suited to the planning function. Another trait is the tendency to plagiarize on others and build these things up into expectations of grandeur. Somewhere along the line, Flash seems to have gone a little "over the edge". He has also learned how to get out of a tight corner. *"Well doesn't that just piss you off"*, he would say, *"give someone some responsibility and they miss-inform you - I'll take care of them immediately"*.

Just recently, Flash learned to use a few personal computer tools. He learned that he could print out and display the numbers that he typed in, at a fraction of the time that it took for him to enter the numbers. After a week he could use one finger from each hand to poke the numbers in. Flash was absolutely amazed when, to his surprise, the spreadsheet package printed them back out in columns. "*Goddammit*" he would say after dragging some unsuspecting victim into his office, "*this high-tech stuff has made me hundreds of times more efficient! I've been thinking about giving the systems group a demo - get their brains working for a change.*" Worse of all, Flash learned how to send the screen contents to someone else's computer by pressing one of the electronic mail function keys. Now he sends junk everywhere and has figured out Google and email. "*Hot damn*" he says, "*Just think of the savings on my walking time and my secretary's typing time! Over fifty years it would sure add up to a lot of time!*"

But Flash's pet project in planning is much more ambitious. He and his manager, Fred Fantasy, together with Bill Blastoff, the Assistant Manager somehow got approval to put together a plan which would project company revenue for the next 100 years. Nobody obviously understood what sort of a commitment they agreed to. Over the years, planning was a place to move people laterally so the group was becoming fairly big. There was Lou Kabbagetop, the Senior Planner, Buzz Bottle, an Intermediate Planner, and Grog Stinky, Harvey Hotshit and Grim Rectum, all "Planners". Including the secretary, Milly DeDilly, the Planning Group consists of 8 people. No wonder a project to keep all these people busy was approved. At any rate, Flash keeps the executive committee informed on his progress. "*The computer*" he says, "*will prove an invaluable and vital asset in our plan. Within a mere two years we will be able to use the scientific method of linear extrapolation on the 30 years of company history to project the future.*" Currently, Flash's staff is deeply immersed in wondering what to do with the 28 points that don't fall on the straight linear line. Fred Fantasy has brought forward a proposal to jointly research the problem of abnormal linear regression with Polyfill Mathematique, a special college near one of the Ontario Plants - at a cost of $150,000.00. So Flash's project has taken on some fairly *significant proportions and impact to the scientific community* as he puts it. Flash is currently preparing a plan to control the "proprietary" results of his findings.

Flash actually used to be the Director of Project Planning until he got into trouble with Angus Steadfast who was at that time the Vice President of Projects.

There was always friction between Angus and Franklin and Flash just happened to get in between. Flash, it seems, was the pawn used by Angus to get Franklin to purchase some reclaimed peat moss bog as "good ranchland" knowing full well it would sink within six months.

He would get Flash to suggest the purchase, hoping that Franklin would buy the land and look stupid. He could then convince Boomer Steadfast to dethrone Franklin. What neither of them knew was that Franklin used to spend lunches there, with one of the buxom meat cutters playing "strip and seek" in the swamps. Needless to say, Franklin was well aware of the peat moss - he used to appreciate its softness when his "seek" was completed.

So when Flash brought forth the idea, Franklin, in his cool style, said it was a good idea and that Flash should write a memo - this would give Flash some of the credit. Well, as usual, Flash panicked, went home, got drunk and beat up the dog. The next day he spilled the beans to Franklin, whereupon Franklin made some fairly indecent threats to Angus. Well, Angus shit-listed Flash but everybody knew the real story.

116

When Frank saved Flash with a new position of VP, everybody felt better. This way Flash was able to survive and even profit, despite the situation and regardless of his abilities. Even when in high school he would cheat on exams. No one could even understand how he ever made it to college - even his parents. How he made it through college and business administration was even more of a mystery. It was said that the key event occurred when Flash happened to rush into one of the wrong rooms in a state of supreme panic. The previous day Flash had fallen off his bicycle, scraping his ankle quite badly. The next day, while waiting for a bus outside the Dean's office, a dog happened to piss on his leg, causing severe pain and immediate panic.

His panic for help resulted in his busting into a room where the Dean was in the process of getting it on with one of Flash's economic professors. It was easy street after that - they couldn't graduate Flash fast enough!

Flash's first job was the result of a similar situation. He had just graduated and was walking through the park feeling pretty good. Having a fairly vigorous game of "pocket billiards" with his privates, he got fairly excited and wasn't watching where he was going - straight into an oncoming biker. The impact panicked Flash and he ran directly into a crotch-high post, severely injuring his crotch. The biker, who happened to be Earl Klutz, the Project Planning Manager at Steadfast, was so dismayed at Flash's agony, that for hours he tried to settle Flash down. Earl finally offered Flash a job as Planner when he realized that Flash was a new graduate.

It was this way that Flash got to be Vice President. He was either at the right place at the right time, someone took pity on him, or he did the wrong thing to get the right results. In his current position, Flash is just a senior pain in the ass. Everybody just hopes that he would leave them alone. Flash, on the other hand, is outwardly disrespectful of anyone who doesn't appreciate talent, progress and good planning. So we all know how high his AQ is.

HERBERT Q. HOYLE

Herbert, known as "work it out Hoyle", has just recently become the Vice President of Engineering. Herb's group is dedicated to overseeing all plant operations and ensuring that all mechanical or other engineering problems are addressed. Herb used to work for old Angus Steadfast, but being a Hawk, Herb couldn't see eye to eye with Angus. Being the belligerent, obnoxious asshole that Angus was, he was threatening to fire Herb because Herb did a respectable job for the President on a little side problem, which he didn't know about. Franklin, who recognized Herb's talents, stepped in to move him into the recently vacant position of Vice President.

To say that Herb was a good engineer was an understatement. Herb was down to the very core, an engineer. Being a fairly quiet individual, soft-spoken and clean cut, Herb wasn't interested in political horseshit - he was there to solve problems. There wasn't a problem that Herb couldn't solve with his training, whether it was mechanical, psychological, economic or religious - it could be reduced to quantifiable and solvable components. Being a mechanical engineer as was Franklin Hardass, it wasn't surprising that they got along well.

Herb has a tendency to sit in his office for days before emerging, in a heap of papers, calculators and computer gizmos everywhere. He has endless pieces of drafting equipment, scattered about his personal computer. Now Herb never argues, he just goes away to work on his computer. His big problem is, however, that he gets sidetracked so easily on new problems. The end result is that he is always trying to solve several

118

problems at one time. Needless to say, he seldom knows what his staff is doing.

Herb came from a poor family who spent all they had to send Herb to school. Being a bit of a spineless pipsqueak anyway, Herb was a natural academic. It was with ease that he headed for the Royal Academy of Wimpy Engineers and graduated with honors in Mechanical Engineering. When Herb graduated from college, he got the job as Project Engineer with Angus Steadfast. At that time Angus was just coming off of his plateau as a good engineer, and had taught Herb quite a lot about project organization and plant design. Herb, of course sucked it all up like a sponge, never being able to use his talents until later when there were no projects. But having an affinity to solve problems, it wasn't surprising that he quietly went outside his department to seek challenges.

Now that Herb is in a position of authority, it is even worse. Just recently, one of the plants was having some mechanical difficulties with one of the auto-retract arms on the castration mechanism. Upon hearing about this, Herb was quick to the rescue, leaving for the plant to gain information, with his portable microcomputer. At the plant, Herb opened his micro, keyed in some numbers, pondered a bit and said the problem was due to the harmonically compounding resonance set in motion by the scrotal impact as it hit the aluminum plate. The next day he explained the situation to Franklin. *"The resonance"*, he said, *"causes a delay in the platinum trigger switch. The result is a random malfunction related entirely to a critical mass of the scrotum"*. Well because Franklin, in his younger days, created the contraption, it was no wonder he was fascinated by Herb's technical prognosis.

For two weeks Herb worked on what the critical mass was and what to do about it. One day Franklin walked into Herb's office to find Herb's secretary, Tina Droop, up on the desk dropping bull scrotums from various marked elevations on the wall - onto an aluminum plate. Herb was peering, unshaven, through a maze of wires, recorders and electronic gizmos trying to measure the impact of the scrotums as they hit. The scrotums were all neatly classified on the bookcase by size. The smell was unreal, even though Herb had a fresh supply sent in daily.

Well that was it! Herb was in Franklin's office for four hours. *"Herb"*, he said, *"your people have been complaining about the smell and they haven't seen you for days! We appreciate your persistence in solving these problems but you are the Vice President - shouldn't you get your staff to look at the problem?"* Herb listened only because he still respected Franklin. He went back and decided to hold daily "exchange" meetings to get on top of things.

Herb is a case where his AQ is well below what his position allows. This is because he has always been too involved in his technical problems. In fact Herb hasn't even met all of the middle management people even though he has been there for over 15 years.

SLINK D. WIRLWIND

Slink is the Vice President of Marketing and Business Development. In this capacity, he controls the search for new business, and the contracts already in place. He also acts in an advisory capacity on matters of economics. Slink is a Hawk trying to be an Eagle. He just wants to climb higher and higher, not caring whom he shits upon as long as they remember it. Now Slink is a silver haired "foxy" looking man, with a flashy but slinky appearance.

He also has developed an incredible ability to present material - with a silver tongue. You can always tell when Slink is giving a presentation - the area outside the boardroom is a tangle of video, audio and various visual aids.

Slink is an Economist from the International School Of Narrow Economic Outlooks. There he learned the First Law of Forecasting, mainly: "*Give them a number or a date but never both*". Having also graduated with an MBA from the Royal School of Business Facades, he remembers the Second Law of Forecasting: "*When you know absolutely nothing about a topic, make your forecasts by asking a carefully selected probability sample of 28 others who also do not know the answer*". In a recent course called "Direction by Misdirection" Slink learned that the best defense is to be offensive. Murk Muddler was also a good student at this course.

Despite Slink's characteristics, he is a mover and a shaker, always itching to try something new - always encouraging even the most ridiculous suggestions. He never seems to stop, he even stands at his desk. He always has piles of airline tickets on his oversized desk. He makes it look like he is always leaving to catch a plane for a big deal. His secretary, Olga Titwopper, has actually resorted to hanging notes and memos on the phones and door knobs, with sticky tape on them, hoping that they will stick to him as he heads for the door. Olga even has an assistant just to do Slink's expense accounts.

But the office of Slink Wirlwind is by far the most interesting. He has special iphones with a microcomputer hooked into just about every local wide and international area data network available. He even has a plotter hooked in and the Chicago Board of Trade's nearest contract prices for live cattle are always displayed on the screen. His desk has a row of baskets labeled IN, OUT, HOLD, DISTRIBUTE and LIBRARY, each with vast piles of economic journals, research papers, memos and price charts. The walls are covered with bar charts, production indices, hog prices, cattle prices and whatever else will fit on the wall. Slink also likes to surround himself with academic weirdo's - the Greymatter Group - so he calls them. "*These people*", Slink reports, "*are essential to the future success of this company - anyway, it keeps your brain from growing moldy*". Recently Slink hired a pretty lady as the Manager of Marketing. She was an economics professor and researcher in the area "Spasmodic Cycle Variations in the Historical Prices of Cattle" so she was an easy choice for Slink.

Years ago Slink used to be the Business Development Manager for a fairly large U.S. based company called International Holding. In this capacity there wasn't much that Slink didn't try to acquire or "hold" as he called it. During his ten years of service, he created a deluge of proposals and contracts that were nearly as staggering as his expenses. One of the reasons that Slink needed several computer at Steadfast was to keep track of his rather extensive (3 books) list of telephone contact numbers and to be able surf the net for research. It was here that Slink learned how to present deals: "*I am in touch with 5 shiploads of non-quota sugar being brought in by Cuban refugees - we must act quickly to set up a disposal company in Florida to acquire and distribute it. We could make millions in a few days.*" he would say, or "*I have reliable contacts in Brazil who can place 18 million pounds of coffee beans in our hands within 48 hours - we can pick up 50 cents a pound easily if we move now.*" were typical Wirlwind proposals concocted from surfing the Net. He knew that if people didn't react within the time period, which was always short, then it wasn't his fault - but the big numbers were always there "*to get things moving*" as Slink would put it.

It was old Boomer Steadfast who hired Slink. They met at a Cattle Buyers Convention in Chicago. Slink had Boomer absolutely thunderstruck as he described how, within the span of two weeks, under his direction, they had purchased, moved and distributed three shiploads of cattle from Australia to the U.S., covering a temporary shortage in the U.S. realizing a handsome 5 million dollars in the deal. Needless to say, Slink insisted that he couldn't divulge too much "confidential" information. So Boomer offered Slink a job as Marketing Manager.

At that time Slink's stay at International Holding had just about run out. He had caused considerable trouble with a few weird deals on which his managers decided to call his bluff so he was happy to leave. Fortunately Slink was with Steadfast through the big bull cycle in the economy. This gave him a chance to expand his staff and his corporate (and personal) living standards. Slink's AQ is quite high because he seldom credits anyone with any intelligence, and in his senior position, has no problem telling anyone so. Moreover, many people just shake their heads when they hear about Slink's incredible deals. Slink knows this so he adds people to his AQ list quickly. Recently, Slink has gotten together with Angus Steadfast to get some new international operations going. Both he and Angus want to be President.

SCOOTER BLASTOFF

Scooter is the Vice President of Operations. With the exception of the Australian Operation, all plants are Scooter's responsibility. Moreover, all of the company's cash flow comes through Scooter from the operations. Scooter is a Hawk, also trying to be an Eagle. In fact, Scooter admits that the presidency is in his line of vision. Admittedly this would be quite possible but Franklin is still years away from retirement and Scoot still has to learn how to treat more people as assholes. In addition, Scoot doesn't yet think that he is an asshole so he would be ill prepared for the position.

Scoot believes firmly in the development of people as he believes equally in rewarding their dedications. Scooter does four main things in his job. He goes to meetings, he scoots around everywhere delegating, he motivates people with his office door closed, and he confuses his secretary whenever possible. Scooter is always on the move, on the phone or in a meeting. He swoops from meeting to meeting picking up things to delegate or he swoops from operation to operation looking for ways to move people around into new positions.

Scoot, at times delegates so many things to so many people that he forgets what he delegated. Just around full moon time, Scoot remembers the odd thing, pulling people into his office or taking them out for lunch to see how they are doing. He also has a tendency to delegate to those who do not work for him, causing considerable confusion. Recently, he hired himself an assistant. Now Scoot can delegate the delegation process.

Scooter doesn't appreciate being crossed, nor does he appreciate lazy assholes - and he doesn't mind telling people directly that they are assholes. He sits at a huge half acre desk, with his feet up showing holes in his shoes, puffing on a big cigar which smells like a mixture of dogshit, hair and sugar, saying: *"Pal, I take care of good people as long as they work well for me."* Typically he says this as he peers through the two-foot stack of memos and reports piled in his IN basket.

It is virtually impossible to say anything because his statements are constantly interspersed with telephone calls. Scooter has a fairly big heart but also a big ego - only his expense account is bigger. Scooter's defense of his expenses is a common expression around the office: *"Hey man, we make big money and make big decisions - when you drive in the fast lane you gotta burn a lotta gas!"*

And fast he is, blasting off from place to place or meeting to meeting. Scoot's secretary has nerves of steel and an uncompromising patience. She is constantly trying to find out where he is, what he has arranged, what luncheon or what meeting he is at - in a never-ending cycle. This is done between setting up socials, trip reservations and various meetings that constantly conflict or are last minute demands.

Scooter has come to believe in the "READY, FIRE, AIM" approach to management. *"Shoot from the lip and piss quickly on crisis fires"*, he says, *"this keeps you sharp and gets the best out of your people"*. Many a time, Scooter has come out of a meeting after negotiating a sale price of beef, then delegated the job (to Engineering and Projects) of coming up with the required operation changes to guarantee a 25% return on investment. Needless to say, the resulting actions are rather chaotic, particularly when the contract has been agreed to and both Engineering and Projects do not report to him. At meetings Scoot is a superb promoter/negotiator, getting to the quick of things rapidly and hanging on like a bulldog with new teeth. Mercilessly he can pound away at contract prices, basing his targets on quick probes on his special iphone/financial calculator. One of his tactics in places that allow it is to stink the room up with his cigars so people are eager to get out of the meeting.

And he always, after a negotiation meeting, can be heard saying: *"Your staff will figure out what to do to accommodate the price we have negotiated. I have complete faith in your people's capabilities. Anyway, what the hell have you got all those high powered people for... bean counting?"*

Scooter came up through one of the plant operations, being hired as one of the Plant Managers. It was a breath of fresh air when Scoot moved to head office. Several of the staff had become unbalanced, drunks and babbling idiots by trying to keep up with

Scooter's unyielding pace. Prior to that Scooter worked at Burnt Meats as an Assistant Manager and Floor Supervisor. Here he got into considerable trouble with his expense account. He had a bad habit of renting hotel accommodations in Las Vegas for the staff once every 3 months. Here he would have information exchange and general motivational sessions - among other things. Being a small operation, Scooter's expense account caused quite an obvious hole in profits.

Scooter was always a keen type, even in school. Having graduated in industrial engineering and also picking up various courses in business administration he always got marks in the upper 10%. So Scoot had the energy to move fairly fast and in some cases he always got the best out of people.

Just recently, however, he and Slink got together and flew down to Brazil to look at buying some operation. They got drunk with some of the government officials and signed a deal to produce incredible amounts of canned meat for half the existing price if the government would turn over the plant for free. Well Franklin knew the area was in dense jungles and in a volatile military area so he hit the roof and lost his cool. Murk Muddler was on the plane the next day to screw the deal up.

NOW SOME OF THE VICTIMS

Well here we have the president and his seven decision makers - the Seven Samurai! We have one Eagle, two Hawks and four Vultures - quite a team. We see that despite what one might think, these executives are just regular well-dressed incompetent guys. But they have obviously picked up new qualities that make them special enough to be at the top and make all those decisions, right? They all have degrees, certificates and diplomas - obviously that helps. They all dress reasonably well - that is an unwritten law. These are certainly not a big deal.

Somewhere they all must have experience that most others don't have - right?

We see that one of them knows how to control meetings and people. We see that one likes to attack people on behalf of the company and one is good at screwing deals up. Another wastes people's time and controls a bunch of useless "has-beens" while the other likes to solve problems. One likes to flash around making and presenting weird deals and the other likes to motivate people by delegating challenges. Four have a tendency to use others and plagiarize while the other two appear constructive but depend on others to produce. And the one at the top controls these decision makers. Strange isn't it?

Well, before we come to any conclusions, let us meet the two new victims from the next lower group - the ones that are about to be judged by this upper echelon.

RANDOLF SNOOPER

Randolf is the Director of Personnel. He is a Kite. These birds are noted for being very swift at stealing from others. They also have a slick appearance. Randolf is one of the slickest, cunning backbiters around. He is concerned with one and only one thing - himself. Randolf got to be the Director because he was Boomer Steadfast's personnel clerk from twenty-five years ago. He has simply outlived everyone in personnel and he has indirectly black-balled any others that appeared to be a threat.

Randolf likes to take credit for other's work and he likes to sneak around spying on others so he can tattle. Randolf, being uneducated, never had great expectations as a professional. When he achieved the height of Director, without the fancy credentials held by others, he became an unbearable creep to listen to. As he became more and more protective of his position, he just became an obnoxious and despicable asshole. In fact, he is an evil corporate Slink, of Pecker species, looking for any opportunity to peck someone if it means an opportunity for him.

Randolf's background is all relatively insignificant since he has really accomplished nothing except to be able to steal, cheat and lie well. Even as a kid he would always try to cheat someone - he was just a bad case right from the start. It was not surprising to see him recognize the power behind Scab Dancer, his boss. He was fast to "attach" himself to Scab, picking up scraps whenever Scab would leave some. His AQ is well beyond his position because he just thinks that everyone is either out to get his job or everyone is just an asshole. His position, therefore, could easily be in jeopardy - a fact that even Randolf recognizes - so he steals and tattles even more to keep his position.

CLEPTO SUPERBYTE

Clepto is the Director of Information Technology. He is a Falcon, trying to be a Hawk. In this position, Clepto is responsible for all information systems within the company. As such, he has, within a few short years, accumulated a small computer operations facility and a group of systems support types. Effectively, Clepto has been primarily involved in the development, implementation and support of various financial reporting systems and office automation. Having had the responsibility of implementing various accounting packages and networking computers at the operations, he has concentrated on the commercial side of information technology and equipment. Just recently, however, Clepto has noticed the appearance of various personal notebooks, iphones and ipads, with a rising interest in the internet and wireless email. Clepto, having watched some of these activities, has stated that the proliferation of these devices based on the random whim of a user, will lead to an unorganized and un-integrated tangle of inefficiency with email transmissions and a proliferation of unorganized files everywhere beyond the corporate control. Scab Dancer has told Clepto to mind his own business - that other department activities are not his concern and that he should focus his attention on the financial area.

Well, Clepto, being a Falcon has always tried to fly higher and is just learning to kill swiftly, but Scab, his boss, is quite a formidable challenge so he has tried to hide his distaste for his boss. Clepto, not believing in Scab's rather selfish approach, has therefore tried to work towards getting away from Mr. Dancer's grip. Worse of all, Clepto has an affinity towards these new iphone devices and some of the more technical areas and electronics, so he would relish being involved with engineering and planning.

In looking at Clepto's background, we find that he is an electrical engineer, having graduated from Hot Circuit College some twelve years ago. Clepto it seems, has always had an insatiable curiosity for connecting wires. Even before college, while back on the farm, Clepto would be seen building various contraptions, cross wiring anything and everything possible. During high school Clepto took the DeFry Electronics Institute correspondence course where he learned to make numerous electrical gismos. He used to drive his father crazy with devices and wires in the barn where Clepto performed many of his experiments. *"Clepto"* his father would scream, *"enough is enough, this goddam barn is a booby trap, I know you are trying to help but if you fry any more chickens with those bloody gismos, the barn is off limits!"* Clepto grew up with an endless imagination and insatiable curiosity. It wasn't surprising to see his imagination increase even more when he got immersed in microcomputers and telecommunications at college. *"Christ"*, he would say, *"this stuff has awesome ramifications towards improving my devices".*

When Clepto graduated, however, he realized that there wasn't much future in gismos or much call in the business world for his interests so he decided to continue his education at a local business administration college. His father was, of course, pleased to see him take something practical and paid for the whole shot. Here Clepto took several courses in Networking and Systems Analysis, as well as Computerized Financial Reporting Systems. It was, in fact, this background that got him the job of Jr. Systems Analyst at a meat packing plant, where he was involved in developing accounts payables and general ledger systems.

It didn't take Clepto long to work his way up to a Supervisor - he was always trying to help others and in fact became quite a good analyst. In his supervisory role however, he had a bit more time to tinker with the computer circuitry. He even refused to have maintenance contracts on the computer equipment since he said he could fix it himself. Needless to say, this was bound to get him in trouble. One day the memory blew on the main computer - from what Clepto said was some transient voltage surges getting through the regulators.

Within seconds he had both regulators apart with oscilloscopes and gismos scattered about. Somehow he got the ground wires and hot wires all screwed up so when he snapped the panel switch, the crackles, blue sparks and smoke were quite impressive. On top of this the smoke triggered the fire alarm and the sprinkler systems. In the chaos, Clepto forgot to disarm the Halon gas system so it blew. In addition the main disk drives crashed, demolishing all of the general ledger and payroll files. The mass evacuation caused several people to get trampled as they panicked. Worse of all, the Plant Manager was, at the time "disciplining his secretary" and did not want to be disturbed - this is what he told the Assistant Manager. It was a fairly interesting sight when the Assistant Manager and his secretary burst into the room to warn them about the fire. Somehow, the boss, with his bare ass sticking up from behind the sofa didn't look like he was disciplining very strongly! Needless to say, Clepto was shit-listed for some time.

So Clepto moved on, finding a new job at Steadfast. Here again Clepto moved forward in a fairly strong, conscientious style, getting the systems moving at the various operations. This led to his promotion as Manager of Systems, just about the time that Scab Dancer took over as his boss. By this time, Clepto's AQ and exposure was growing steadily.

He was always learning quietly, becoming quite polished in his dealings with people and always there to tackle a problem. This was the time when his staff and empire grew, getting all operations and head office well entrenched into fairly constructive computerization.

Clepto, it seems, also had an insatiable yearning for knowledge about corporations and human behavior. He was a constant reader, ingesting the most peculiar information as if by osmosis. He was always carrying around books such as Management Mania, Instrumental Conditioning for Executives, Tactical Manipulation, and Backroom Brawling. In addition, he would rarely miss an opportunity to take a seminar or courses on similar topics.

In this way, Clepto was always able to deal with the corporate cultures and the ever-changing climate. With more idle time on his hands he also began to read multitudes of technical information, becoming a virtual storehouse of "high tech" ideas in the area of communications and computing. But Clepto had also learned how to get things done - he knew that he had to write something or present something in such a way as to make Scab look good - this procedure, he realized would produce benefits which would rub off downwards to him. So even though he didn't like Scab, it didn't take long to get the promotion to Director of Information Technology. He even convinced Scab to hire Garfle Greymatter, a research type to study the areas of micro-telecommunications. The idea was to develop an automated network of telecommunicated consolidated financial reporting for Scab.

Clepto also realized that Scab was an obstacle to his corporate growth. Why shouldn't the company have a Vice President of Information Technology? It was just as important a function as planning or projects. His AQ, by this time was fairly high - ready to move into disequilibrium if he didn't get a new position. So it was not surprising to see increased friction and minor disagreements between Clepto and Scab. Scab being a shrewd vulture has sensed that he might start watching Clepto more carefully.

Well, these are our two new heroes (or victims) who are to present their material to the executive committee. Both have a personal interest, in getting approval for their projects, not an unusual situation. The third topic and presentation is from the two characters already known to us, mainly Angus Steadfast and Slink Wirlwind. The presentation to them is "old hat" but their interests and motives are nevertheless the same - just at a higher level.

10

THE BIG EXECUTIVE MEETING

The meeting has been scheduled for 9:00 am to 11:00 am. To the "Seven Samurai" it is just another meeting. In accordance with company procedure, the final reports on the topics have been circulated to all attendees two weeks in advance of the meeting. Most have read the "Executive Summary" and have scanned the contents in some attempt to isolate little items to pick at during the meeting.

The morning gathering has started as usual, with the executives scattered about the plush teak-walled boardroom. Most are seated, slurping their morning coffee while Clepto and Randolf pretend not to be nervous. Murk, in his usual crassness waddles over to Clepto and snorts *"Hi there Clep, ya big arsehole, ha ha ha... did you hear what one nut said to the other?"* Clepto, being quite embarrassed, and knowing that executive eyes were upon him, quietly replied: *"Sorry Murk, I don't"* and quickly sat down. Murk's response seemed to be incredibly loud to Clepto: *"Why should we hang when it was slim who did the shooting!"* replied

Murk as he started to heave and guffaw with laughter. Well Angus started to also laugh encouraging Murk even more, causing Murk to lose control of his posterior sphincter muscle and he let loose a resounding gaseous emission that instantly permeated the boardroom air. Clepto, not experienced in these matters of dealing with Murk was horrified but it was a bit funny to see this gross character alternating short gas bursts with wheezing snorts of laughter. As he began to chuckle and gag from the smell that now filled the boardroom, in walked Franklin. *"Thank God I sat down and Hardass didn't see me with this asshole"*, Clepto said to himself, trying to appear as if he was studying his papers. Murk nearly choked on the two jelly donuts that he was trying to stuff in his mouth, causing one last gas bubble to escape from his $300 pants. The instant silence was so awesome that you could hear a feather drop. You could almost cut the air with a knife.

"Good morning to you Frank" slurped Randolf Snooper, as everyone glanced at each other as if to say, *"who is this asshole kidding?"* With the smell still fairly heavy, Franklin's greeting was predictable: *"Good morning gentlemen"*, he cracked, *"I trust that you have enjoyed your morning entertainment and are all sufficiently prepared to deal with the matters at hand. I am sure that you have all met Mr. Snooper and Mr. Superbyte so I will, if Murk is finished with his performance, direct your attention to the items on the agenda."*

At this point it will be noticed how quickly Franklin took over the meeting, bringing some order to it and making everyone look silly at the same time - in two simple sentences. Let us now follow the proceedings:

HARDASS *"Gentlemen, we will first deal with item number 1 on the agenda. This deals with the proposal to implement an Enhanced World Wide Computerized Telecommunications*

Network. Mr. Clepto Superbyte of the Information Technology Group will summarize the proposal for us all."

SUPERBYTE *"The estimate for the project is set before you in Appendix 27. For a total cost of 4 million dollars we will implement high speed computerized data, voice and image processing between all existing and future operations throughout the world. This will greatly increase the management control and reporting methods. You have all no doubt seen the general architecture of the network in Figure 237 that includes a synchronized transitional capability. The project estimates and the potential prototype prosthesis have been further analyzed by Dr. U. R. Rippedoff, our consulting communications engineer for Katchem & Rippem Associates of Murkywater, Illinois. These findings, included in Appendix 937 also contain comments on one of the contending issues - that of satellite imagery transmission using convex transients. As a follow-up, we have included the findings of Professor Spacey Klutz of the Faculty of Satellite Engineering at the University of Blastemoff. He assures us in his report that laser optic technology is already at an advanced stage and that polarity propagation proposition is already in fact a proven theory. This means that our estimates as to the benefits could potentially be grossly under rated. We do, however, remain conservative. We also submit a report by Dr. Kinky Flutter that confirms our submission that radio wave document transmission and videotext integration modules are already available. This is included in Appendix 144. In summary, we are in a position to take advantage of new breakthroughs in technology and at the same time get a decent rate of return on the investment and enhance company productivity. This most certainly is consistent with Mr. Dancer's concern of ever improvement in matters of financial reporting and management control. I would be pleased at this time to answer any questions that the members of the committee might have."*

HARDASS *"Thank you Clepto for a very lucid and thorough explanation of the proposal. I would now invite members to give us their views. Flash, you have recently acquired new icomputers, perhaps you can offer some criticism."*

Notice that Hardass is purposely pitting the mouthy Mr. Spreadsheet against Clepto to find out what each of them is made of. He wants to use either one to credit or discredit the other...

SPREADSHEET *"Frank, I wish to express my concern over commitments in regards to our consultants on this proposal. I wish that I had as much confidence in the findings and estimates. We should have solicited the advice of a local consultant for a more concrete evaluation and we could have avoided such wide guesses on the availability or status of laser optics. Moreover, Dr. Klutz, I understand is of a somewhat suspicious reputation."*

SUPERBYTE *"Mr. Dancer has already expressed such a concern and it is for this reason that we remain conservative on benefits and harsh on estimates. It should be noted that local consultants are not even registered members of the International Laser Association and as such cannot be classified as consultants on the topic. In any case, the success is not contingent upon this aspect. As to Dr. Klutz, the appendix contains a list of his technical papers as reference material. You have obviously assessed his theories to make such a conclusion."*

SPREADSHEET *"What page is that on?"*

Obviously Flash just lost his luster and Franklin has learned two things. Clepto knows what he is talking about and Flash doesn't. So much for the Planning Group - now what about this new superstar against Engineering.

HARDASS *"Herb, perhaps you can offer some of your comments on this topic."*

Now Herb is perhaps closer to technology than any of the other Samurai and he is probably the only one who has any clue about what is being discussed. In fact he could possibly give Clepto considerable static but he has just witnessed Flash being reduced rather quickly in a technical attack. In reality Herb knows just enough to know that he does not know enough to confront Clepto. Herb even knows about Dr. Klutz being fired from his job in industry when he hot-wired the Xerox machines with the telephones and some state of the art monitors in order to transmit copies. The company is still fighting legal battles over the lawsuits, which resulted from the many fried ears. And Dr. Rippedoff was sued only last year for a scam involving the sale of laser controlled toilet flushers. Herb knows that much of what is proposed is partly science fiction but he is not prepared to go into lengthy discussions to justify it. Moreover, he also knows that many talented people are a little weird so why pick on Klutz and Rippedoff? In addition, Herb, remember, is a Hawk, so he likes progress and new horizons. It would be smart, therefore, to take a positive deflection of the matter.

HOYLE *"The project represents a considerable undertaking and I think Clepto has addressed the major issues in a constructive and thorough manner. I think it is healthy to encourage projects which make use of new technology particularly when there are numerous benefits."*

HARDASS *"Thank you Herb. Now gentlemen, are we all satisfied on the business of costs and benefits?"*

Obviously Franklin is interested in an explanation or a confrontation on benefits. This is, of course, Scab Dancer's queue. Now, as we know, Scab is Clepto's boss and Clepto very cleverly, has involved Scab by having him provide some critical guidelines in the proposal. Moreover, finance people know only one word, mainly 'NO' and in this respect Scab is hardly an exception. Being a Vulture, he must pick carefully to identify the state of his possible victim, but also take care not to injure his contribution. This could be an opportunity to look cool and test his boy at the same time.

DANCER "*Considerable analysis has been done in the area of cost-benefit. Clepto has assured me that this is the case and that his reputation stands on his conclusions. It would be beneficial to all at this time, given the size of the capital outlay, to have Clepto give a concise summary of the cost/benefit sections.*"

Notice how Scab has used Franklin's tactics to pass the buck over to Clepto. He avoids the question and he wants to see how healthy Clepto is. Notice also, how he has nicely committed Clepto's reputation (not his) if he should fail. Superbyte, however, is no dummy and being a Falcon he can move fast. So he takes up his calling.

SUPERBYTE "*I refer you all to page 12 of the Executive Overview and pages 131 to 160 which deals explicitly with costs. You will see a detailed breakdown and explanation of each item and function in the project. This also includes the manpower requirements as shown in a critical path network. We will need at least one hour to go through this. I assume that everyone had enough time to study this and therefore will query specific items so as to minimize wasted time.*"

"*The benefits are enumerated in Section 10 and summarized as 32 points in the executive overview. Effectively, the planned replacement of video, audio, image, data and document devices at a cost of $4,000,000 will yield a 35% reduction in executive* response time. According to Shifty Statistics Inc., an estimate of 20% decrease on plant operating costs is conservative because of more timely and accurate financial reporting. At an estimated growth rate of 12.7% per year and using a sum of digits depreciation scheme on capitalized equipment we attain a rate of return of 31% over five years with payback in 3 years of project startup. I have devoted a complete section to this important segment and Mr. Dancer has verified its accuracy. Would you like to review each item?"

DANCER *"Thank you Clepto, for a very thorough summary. I think that everyone will agree that we in the Finance Department always do our homework."*

It will be noticed how Scab is quick to grab some credit when Clepto comes out as being alive and well on the issues of finance. Had Clepto faltered, it would have undoubtedly been a different story. The buzzards and vultures would have had their signal to attack. Scab would have attacked him for leading him astray. Also, it is quite obvious that Scab has picked up some meeting tactics from Franklin.

HARDASS *"Very well, what about you Murk, are there any legal ramifications involved?"*

MUDDLER *"I've had my top man Lardo Billowgroin research this matter thoroughly. It would appear that whereas no precedent has hereto been set forth and hence previously pushed back, all satellite transmission offers no contrarium to recognized copyright cases. Any image copy falls under the international jurisdiction of Xeroxio Bandido and upto and heretoforwith has no substance in Law."*

HARDASS *"Thank you Murk for your rather opaque answer. If you gentlemen have no further questions? From your silence I* *take it that you are all in agreement? Clepto, I have a final question for you. It appears that you have put together a thorough report and that you are wholly committed to the completion of the program and its success, but how are we assured that the project will be controlled and reported regularly to us so that budget and time constraints are adhered to?"*

At this point everyone murmurs agreement as all members start to rustle their papers, pretending that they had the same question written down.

SUPERBYTE *"Yes Sir, you have my firm commitment. In matters of budget control, Scab has, I believe, assured us that his accounting staff already has a system in place to do this. This must have been the case with other projects."*

Actually, Clepto knew of the disaster that occurred with the Australian project so he quite smoothly pushed the question and responsibility over to Scab. Scab, caught quite off guard, recovered himself quickly. He would be on Oscar Ostrich's case immediately to make sure everything was in place in the accounting department.

DANCER *"Yes, my staff has assured me that all systems are ready to monitor and report according to your needs."*

HARDASS "Thank you gentlemen, the project is hereby approved. I will expect a report on progress at the next meeting."

Exactly five minutes have been spent to approve a $4,000,000 project. But many things have occurred in such a short time. Even though the topic is well beyond all those in attendance, Franklin has managed to extract agreement, consensus, commitment and accountability without knowing details or giving opinions. In addition, he has had a pretty good indication of performance and capabilities. In fact, it doesn't really matter how much of the Appendices are unadulterated crap, for he sees a good thorough presentation of considerable thought and volume and he has the proper commitments and controls in place. So everything went rapidly because no one was familiar with the topic and all you could go on was costs, benefits, accountability and faith. And Superbyte handled himself well, even getting a dig at his boss and reducing the V.P. of Planning to a mumbler.

Clepto had volumes of crap organized professionally into an impressive binder, with all the appropriate summaries and sections circulated well before the meeting. His presentation was a concise summary of technical words, meaningless jargon modifiers and key executive related interests such as benefits, costs, paybacks, etc. What is also noteworthy is that Clepto is not really a threat to anyone (yet), so although everyone is out to pick and poke at his proposal, it is in the name of progress and to see what he is made of. The jockeying is not too lethal at this point, although Flash did regret his minor attack.

The next situation is somewhat similar in this respect but Randolf is not really as interested in going upwards in the company as he is in staying where he is. Secondly, the topic is of a much more widely understood nature. Some of the members have, as yet, said nothing, so they would like to demonstrate that they are pulling their weight.

HARDASS *"With reference, gentlemen, to item number 2 on our agenda, recommendations have been brought forward by Randolf Snooper, our Director of Personnel, to standardize on all bathroom tissue within executive and staff washrooms. Randolf, we will call on you to enlighten us in this matter."*

SNOOPER *"I have had my subordinate staff members conduct the study which is tabled before you. Our current situation is that* we have 10 executive washrooms here at head office and 2 in each of the plants. These washrooms are supplied with superior tensile strength tissue of the scenic variety while the other 20 public washrooms contain the poorer quality paper that is scratchy and has a suspicious strength. The costs are $40.00 and $200.00 per month for executive and public facilities. The recommendation brought forward is that there must be a standardization of this tissue."

Randolf is quite abruptly interrupted by Angus Steadfast and Murk Muddler...

STEADFAST *"Surely this is outrageous! That is a ridiculous amount of toilet paper!"*

MUDDLER *"I agree. These bloody workers never seem to be satisfied. What the hell do they want and how the hell did all this get started?"*

SNOOPER *"We must all have one type of paper. If it is the executive type paper then the net increase will be $40.00 per month or $480.00 per year. In discussions with Brenda Breeder and Pomp Crotchley, my staff members, it has come to my attention that we have had repeated complaints by staff members which point to discriminatory practices on the part of management. Several appear to have detected the difference in tissue quality. In addition, Crotchley, my Supervisor of Personnel has informed me that there are mounting requests to provide abrasive, higher cost soaps in order to wash brown stains from the finger tips. It is our recommendation that all paper be standardized to the lower cost variety. The cost savings will offset the soap costs and show the staff that we care. More important, we will avert the cost of an employee walkout should this become more serious."*

STEADFAST "*I must concur with Murk. How did such information become staff knowledge? Is security not responsible for this? Why the hell are these people wandering around in our washroom facilities? Who is responsible for this?*"

DANCER "*My staff assures me that they have done their jobs. We are always conscious of tight security on such matters. It is quite obvious that you, gentlemen, need to practice more discretion on how, and with whom, you share your facilities.*"

BLASTOFF "*Regardless of the situation, I find it hard to believe that we spend so much money on toilet paper. My wife buys good paper for 25 cents a roll.*"

STEADFAST "*Scoot, that's not relevant, we can't have this. The next thing you know Personnel and the staff will be telling us what color of ass-wipe we should use.*"

We now have a fairly heated discussion taking place. Undoubtedly the executives feel an invasion on their privacy and perhaps even an invasion on their "privates". They probably can feel that scratch of cheap paper. So far Franklin hasn't even had a chance to break in. He sees Herb working on his calculator so he speaks loudly.

HARDASS "*Gentlemen, let us acknowledge and face the real issues at hand. This is to be dealt with in a logical manner. Randolf, perhaps you could elaborate upon these figures which are included in the Executive Overview.*"

SNOOPER "*By all means, Frank. The figures are based upon an average use of 2 rolls per month in the executive washrooms of which there are 10 here, and based upon 20 rolls per month in each of the 20 staff washrooms. The executive rolls cost $2.00 each while the other rolls cost 50 cents each.*"

HOYLE *"My calculations show that to replace the public rolls would yield a net of $150 per roll for 20 rolls. This is a net increase of $30.00 per month for each washroom or $600 per month in total. With 80 staff members, we are using 400 rolls a month, or at some 888 wipe panels per roll this amounts to 355,200 wipes per month. We work an average of 7 hours a day for 20 days. This means that someone is wiping his ass every 1.4189 seconds. That seems excessive to me. You said that the net gain was $40.00 per month. Have I misunderstood something?"*

SNOOPER *"On page 12 of the report, you will see that I have used an efficiency factor of 3 to 1. That is, because of the flimsy quality of the staff paper, approximately 3 times as much paper is required to produce the same quality of wipe as the executive type. We have included in Appendix 2 a report from the University where extensive material strength analysis tests were carried out to verify this factor. This means that whereas 400 rolls per month are now being used, only 133 rolls of the executive paper is required."*

HOYLE *"That still means that at a net of $1.40 per roll you are still at $200 per month, not $40.00 per month."*

SPREADSHEET *"And in fact, if we should change executive paper, our costs would be for 60 rolls rather than 20 and the cost would be $30.00 per month rather than the current $40.00 per month. Anyway, what guarantee have you that the staff will automatically use the new paper in accordance with a tensile strength? If they continue to use the same amount, they will triple that cost."*

DANCER *"Randolf, there appears to be a discrepancy here on the monthly costs. These numbers appear to be different from those presented for my approval in the earlier report."*

SNOOPER *"Pomp Crotchley assured me that these figures were correct. Shall I call him in?"*

DANCER *"No, we do not have the time now, perhaps we should move on."*

BLASTOFF *"It was mentioned that such action could avert an employee walkout. Has someone been delegated the responsibility to study the impact of this in terms of costs?"*

STEADFAST *"I agree with Scoot, and what is the policy in the plants? What do they do? What we do here will establish a precedent throughout the company - what about the cost of that?"*

HOYLE *"I am still not happy about the frequency of use - people must be wiping their asses constantly."*

WIRLWIND *"I am not satisfied with the prices of tissue. Surely with volumes such as this we could get better prices or volume discounts. Did you conduct a price survey?"*

MUDDLER *"There ain't no goddam precedents that allow these non-union ass-wipers to tell us what to do. If these jerkoffs walk out we can legally fire their asses."*

SNOOPER *"I will not be held responsible for the consequences of a walkout should people act upon such discrimination."*

Now what is transpiring here is a fairly heavy debate quickly headed for a fairly hot emotional exchange. Whereas, in the first topic, most members knew little about computers and telecommunications, toilet paper and its uses is a topic very dear to all of them and they are all, needless to say, experts on the topic. Moreover, the possibility of standardizing to thin scratchy paper is not a palatable idea. So everyone offers questions freely and furiously creating a lengthy debate, without Franklin's need to probe indirectly. Also, because the topic affects everyone, and it is within everyone's comprehension, the amount of money involved is totally irrelevant. Well, after about 20 more minutes of this, Randolf's plan is not looking too good and the whole session borders on the ridiculous. Franklin finally comes to the rescue.

HARDASS *"It seems, gentlemen, that we need additional information before any decisions can be made. While you senior gentlemen have been shouting at each other, I have noted a total of six questionable areas. There is the business of correct figures, price surveys, company policy, walkout possibility/impact, frequency of use and new use characteristics. Are there any comments?"*

HOYLE *"It would seem in order to substitute the stronger paper in a few public locations to study whether wiping habits change."*

HARDASS *"A good suggestion Herb. Randolf, we have reserved decisions until the noted areas are addressed. We will deal with the topic at a subsequent meeting. We will now take a quick break before we deal with the third item."*

At this point, Slink Wirlwind heads out of the boardroom with Angus. Outside, various audiovisual devices have been delivered for Slink's presentation. Their proposal, being a joint effort is next up. They have decided to "bottom line" their proposal as much as possible showing only relevant material and facts (as they see them). Slink is to cover the introduction while Angus is to cover financial impacts.

But we have a new entry to the meeting - old Boomer Steadfast, the owner. Angus, of course had made sure that his uncle knew about this proposal and he had aroused the old bugger's curiosity. *"I don't think Franklin can handle this type of growth."* he told his uncle, *"We are going to need some fairly serious decisions to be made here and Frank won't admit that he needs your help."* So Angus convinced Boomer to go to the meeting - to listen and check up on Franklin, but it would be best not to announce the arrival. Well the arrival signal was to let Boomer know when the coffee break was, so he could hobble down from his penthouse office.

So in hobbled Boomer, picking away at the ass of his pants. *"Hi there boys"* he crackled, *"thought I'd drop down to see some action, heh, heh, heh,"* he chortled, as he sat down in his reclining chair. *"Why hello Boomer "* said Franklin, with surprise, *"we were about to get a presentation on a new venture - perhaps you want to stay - let me introduce you to some of these new faces"*. *"So far so good"* thought Angus, *"I can't believe the old fart actually remembered and made it."* After a few minutes, things finally settled down and Franklin boomed out his statement.

HARDASS *"Gentlemen, we will now address item 3 which is a joint proposal by Slink and Angus to set up new plant operations.*

Now, although Slink and Angus have circulated a report prior to the meeting, this report is fairly sketchy on supporting details. Being fairly senior, they do not feel that the need for detail is important - the staff can be told to work out the required details at any point. All they need is for Frank, Herb, Scooter and Scab to agree and they can launch the project. As such, their plan is virtually a scam - being more of a promotional campaign to "get the ball rolling" as they put it. As it stands, Angus and Slink have been to Colombia three times, spending a few weeks each time "promoting the deal". The deal started when Angus got quite pissed at Slink's place and they started to exchange lies. Angus listened to one of Slink's big deals in South America. *"Shit man,"* Angus told Slink *"that deal would have gone through if I was in control - I would build a goddam profitable plant in the jungles if I had to!"* Well one thing led to another and it wasn't long before Slink and Angus were forming a vast empire in South America. It was only natural that they would locate some of Slink's old contacts and make a "reconnaissance" trip to Colombia.

The bullshit and booze that was passed between Slink, Angus and the contacts in Bogota, Colombia was indeed something for history to make note of. The potential deals and opportunities that were fabricated were incredible. And the expense accounts were equally incredible. But now it was time to report all the findings and bring the company into a *"new era of growth and prosperity"*, as they put it. Let's follow their ploy.

WIRLWIND *"Gentlemen, you have before you our preliminary assessment and proposal for a new operation in Colombia. This is only the start of an incredible scenario, which can open new and vast international opportunities for this company... Angus, could you turn the lights down please... you will all see from this slide of the projected consolidated cash flow what the impact of this could be if we act quickly... By the year 2015 we could be a one billion dollar a year company, with a complete international exposure. In this next slide you will see that we have covered four major considerations - those of supply, demand, economics and politics. In consideration of the supply, you will see in this aerial shot, some 125,000 acres of land with an estimated 40,000 head of cattle and substantial housing facilities. These shots show the vast waterways, grazing land and lakes on the*

148

land, near Maicao. We have negotiated a contract with the Colombian officials to purchase this land from them - a copy of the letter is in the report. On the demand side, I have had my staff, under the direction of Donna Dingdong, prepare these exponential projections of meat and meat product demand in both Colombia and Venezuela over the next 20 years. These are based upon continued population growth and existing demands. You will note the "hot area" as we call it where the demand accelerates away from supply, with a tenfold impact on prices. The economics, with a capital cost of $125,000,000 results in the cash flow as seen on the first slide. Politically we have spent much time with government officials and we have their complete support. This slide was taken at the banquet held for us at the president's home where all chief military and government officials gave us their support. The Bogota officials have agreed to sell us their government-controlled operation at bargain prices, conditional upon the plant being built in Santa Marta."

By this time, Boomer has fallen asleep, his snores rattling his false teeth, with the odd squeaky fart sneaking its way out between snorts. Although the noise and smell are somewhat unnerving, the deluge of slides of the tropical coastline along the Caribbean that Slink is now showing, has captured everyone's interest. The selfish thoughts of getting involved in this project are flipping through everyone's minds. Closing with some tantalizing shots of resort areas and some of the exotic nightlife, Slink hands off to Angus.

STEADFAST *"We have estimated the plant to cost $60,000,000 to build at Santa Marta over a period of 1½ years. The head office facility would be built at Riohacha for a further cost of $5,000,000. The existing ranch operation would cost $35,000,000. Adding a 25% contingency, our total estimate for capital cost is $125,000,000. Our operating costs at the ranch would bottom line at $0.25 per pound live weight while the plant*

149

would cost a further $0.35 per pound of processed meat. At a 80% waste to processed ratio the ranch operation costs convert to $0.375 per pound of processed meat. Our calculations indicate $0.05 per pound for head office overhead and $0.05 for transportation. According to local prices our range of products would retail at an average weighted composite of $1.90 per pound of processed product. We would expect to double our herd within the construction period so that a minimum of 30,000 head would be available upon start up. Since the plant capacity has been sized at 60,000 per year, we could double revenue within 3 years. The Colombian officials guarantee large cattle on the ranch, at an average weight of 1,200 pounds per head. At 60% waste and by-products we can process 14,400,000 pounds in the first year. With a profit of $1.075 per pound we can realize $15,480,000 in the first year. This could be doubled to $30,000,000 net profit in the second year of operation."

WIRLWIND "With a capital cost of 125 million and considering the time value of money, at the net profit scenario as shown by Angus, we are looking at 30% rate of return after a mere five years. The Colombian officials have indicated that there are a further 3 more such opportunities scattered throughout Colombia which we would take over in two-year increments. Over the decade you will see the company cash flow double. The expansion into Venezuela would be natural."

STEADFAST "The Colombian officials indicate that they have four other buyers for this ranch which is the key to our move into Colombia. We must therefore act quickly."

So what we have here is a fairly respectable idea to expand the company. The truth of the matter is that the Colombians are trying to suck some new capital into their country and bail out of a bad operation. They have also made sure that numerous "provisions" and "services" are to be provided as part of the deal.

But despite all this, Angus and Slink have indicated the preliminary nature of the proposal and there could be some merit in all this.

HARDASS *"Thank you gentlemen for a fast moving presentation. I can now see what you have been working on over the last six months. We will now open the meeting up for questions. Boomer what do you think about this?"*

Frank's voice startled Old Boomer and he almost choked as he awoke. Boomer had become fairly senile but he still could react fairly fast.

BOOMER *"Damn good work lads... good presentation... what's it gonna cost us this time?"*

STEADFAST *"We require 35 million to purchase the ranch, with a further 90 million spent over the next 1½ years."*

DANCER *"I see nothing in your proposal on taxes. What consideration is there for taxes and the potential impact on cash flow? And what of the movement of capital out of Colombia?"*

WIRLWIND *"The Colombian government has assured us that they will not tax us for the first five years so that we can establish a base of operation. We have asked for a letter to verify this. They have also stated that they will not interfere with money movement as long as we re-invest all capital within the five-year period. We must negotiate for anything thereafter."*

BLASTOFF *"You propose to maintain operating costs of $0.34 per processed pound. This cost is what our best plant in the best of conditions is costing us. The environmental and economic conditions are radically different in Colombia. Are you not a bit optimistic on your operating costs?"*

WIRLWIND *"The labor market is much cheaper by about one half and the plant is at a sea port. In fact the main port of Maracaibo in Venezuela is also close. With labor cheaper and materials readily accessible from the U.S., we feel our estimates conservative. We have provided contingencies of 25% on capital costs and 6 months on construction."*

HOYLE *"Angus, on what did you base your construction costs - they seem a little loose at this time. From where did you get the cost of materials. Did you take one of our plant layouts and solicit quotes from a local Colombian contractor?"*

STEADFAST *"Herb, I built plants when you were still playing with yourself in high school. If you can recall some history, Boomer and I built the plants and the company. But to answer your question, we extrapolated the cost of the last construction, adding an inflation factor of 12% per year..."*

MUDDLER *"I don't see nothing here that will, after our undertaking of the commitments in question, force these assholes in Colombia to legally bind themselves. They probably wipe their asses with these letters."*

WIRLWIND *"Murk, if you knew anything about politics and international law, I would be willing to listen. Your expertise is hardly in the judgment of international law. These gentlemen have issued their intents and this should be good enough for now. Anyway if we need to bail out I am sure we can send you down to screw the deal up."*

MUDDLER *"Where does a piss-assed fucking used car salesman like you get off telling me about screw ups. You remember when..."*

SPREADSHEET *"We haven't talked about a plan, although you gentlemen must have one in mind. I don't see a critical path of events in your report."*

STEADFAST *"Flash, only you would say something so stupid at this time. Did you not read the word preliminary on the report. What the hell do we need a critical path for when we are making a general proposal?"*

SPREADSHEET *"Well all I hear is a bunch of general horseshit with no plan of action. How do you expect to get my support on this?"*

STEADFAST *"Flash, your support is of virtually no significance to our proposal. Your significance is to play king keeper to those deadbeats and drunks in your department. If you don't recognize the opportunities for this company then clearly you are an asshole."*

We are getting into some fairly heavy discussion here. Even Boomer is wide awake since it has become too noisy to snooze. Anyway, he likes the action - he hasn't had this much fun for a long time. But both Boomer and Franklin have been quiet. Each participant has attempted to confront Angus or Slink on a particular issue but they have failed each time. Although the attacks are becoming more emotional and less relevant, they are nevertheless attempting to convey an important aspect of a corporate concern. Angus and Slink have quite clearly taken control, even though it has been personal emotionalism, and with Boomer there to approve the deal, there seems to be little in their way. All this time, Clepto and Randolf have been hiding in their chairs, hoping and praying that no one takes notice of them. They are, needless to say, amazed at the proceedings.

But all this time Franklin has said little. He has in fact, lost control and both Angus and Slink are slowly dismantling the Vice Presidents. He notes, however, that the project may indeed have merit and even potential. He sees that old Boomer is starting to smile and giggle wryly when Angus shits on one of the others. So Franklin Hardass, the Chief Executive Officer and high-flying Eagle that he is, has to attack before he gets wounded himself.

Both Angus and Slink are treating the VP's like assholes and are getting away with it. They have yet to get Franklin. But guess who has been making some notes through the performances?

HARDASS *"I have tried to listen objectively to the proceedings while you gentlemen, if I can use the term loosely, continue with emotional and loose conjectures. As I understand the situation, and Boomer, you can correct me, Angus and Slink are, in a preliminary proposal, asking us to put up $35,000,000 for a ranch operation, which in turn creates the immediate liability of a further $65,000,000. To this they add $25,000,000 for contingencies as they put it, which would cover errors. They have, in order to balance this "preliminary expenditure" set before us an impressive cash flow projection based upon extrapolations, incomplete and vague estimates together with promises from a government both unstable and untrustworthy in their dealings with foreign investment. Angus, you have not built a plant for at least a decade and as Herb will acknowledge, plant technology, requirements and costs are far different now. We have nothing to show us whether the ranch is a good investment or even if it really exists. The fact that it is situated in hostile Indian country where rustling and high mortality rates are common is obviously of minor concern. I am still dismayed at how you related our local operating costs to those in Colombia with a "flick of the pencil". And I wish that I had your confidence on the tax guarantee,* *particularly when they change governments so rapidly. I see absolutely nothing that we could take to a banker."*

Frank obviously made his move. He has attacked them both directly and attempted to give the other VP's their credibility back - therefore indirectly getting their support if a counter-attack is launched by Angus and Slink. But while the air is thick with cold silence, Franklin moves swiftly in for the kill, using to the fullest extent his power as Chief Executive.

HARDASS *"We cannot approve any expenditures of 35 million at this time since it causes a chain reaction of additional liabilities which are based upon sketchy information. Your presentation is purely so much horffle, wind and smoke. Since, however, I do see some merit to the idea, it would perhaps be more in order to lay out an evaluation plan to investigate and report the important aspects. We have people dealing in land costs. We need to look at plant designs and solicit local estimates as Herb suggests. A labor and marketing survey needs to be done and we need more concrete agreements with the government. We need to look at the environmental and political aspects of such operations. Then we require a project plan with detailed cost estimates. We have the departments to analyze this properly and thoroughly. I would suggest that you all get together and come up with a plan which identifies areas of responsibilities, costs and timing of such an initial undertaking. You all have staff that are skilled in each area where more details are required. When this is laid out, Boomer and I will review it. Are there any questions?"*

After this there is little that can be said without being emotional. Angus and Slink have been reduced to mere players rather than leaders. In fact if they had been smart, they would have proposed that a study be conducted first - and not try to take over. But Angus is not finished:

STEADFAST *"Let it be noted that should this deal fall through because we were not able to act fast enough, you are solely responsible for the consequences."*

HARDASS *"I would feel happier about saving the company from a bad decision rather than suffering the consequences, as you put it, of some sketchy projections. You and Slink are the key ingredients to attaining the deal in written form - we cannot act without this - but we must know the type of commitment we are to be involved in. Boomer, how do you feel about this?"*

BOOMER *"There is no question that I agree, Frank. We can't piss away money on sketchy deals."*

So Angus tried to recover himself one more time with little success. Not only that, the old man was lost as a potential supporter as well.

HARDASS *"Thank you gentlemen for your attendance. We will address the new submissions in two weeks."*

Well this is the way things happen at the top of the corporate pyramid. If it looks fairly silly, it's because, in most cases, it really is. These are just normal incompetent professionals who know little if nothing about the technical details upon which they must make decisions.

The jockeying for position and AQ interaction is as common as the boardroom itself. What have we learned from all this? Let's wait until we look at the AQ tools that these executives use to survive with later on. You will recognize them when they are revealed to you.

SO WHAT'S THE BIG DEAL ABOUT MEETINGS?

You may ask at this point: "So what? What is the big deal about these executives and their decision making meetings?" The big deal is simply that this is where the big deals are made, by little fellows not unlike the ones you just met. The other big deal is that these fellows don't really know much about the details on which they are making decisions. In fact, the more detailed they get the stupider they look - who really cares about the tensile strength of ass wipe? More often than not, AQ'ISM virus gravitates to ego and position conflicts.

If you can recall what was said at the beginning of the chapter, it was stated that *"Meetings bring together a group of incompetent assholes that attempt to exchange and present ever-deteriorating information in such a way as to impress each other so they can become bigger assholes and effect company profits".* This was a fairly strong statement but having watched this executive meeting, just think about your own meetings and see if there is any similarity. Another big deal is that these executives spend more than half of their corporate life in these meetings where they make decisions on things they appear to know little about. Do you think, given the amount of time spent in meetings that they have developed a toolbox of their favorite tools to protect profits and their positions? Do you think these may have anything to do with their AQ's and keeping them healthy?

SO WHAT'S THE SECRETS?

If we look more closely at the meeting, we see that Franklin Hardass had the power. Not only had he the formal power of the president but he also had the informal power to maintain order and control. So which comes first - presidency or ability to maintain order? We see that the attendees certainly had a few things in common.

- They had some formal education
- They had, in their climb upwards, managed to get through each of the bottom two levels by some special accomplishment
- They have worked a long time so they are fairly senior
- Their AQ's are fairly high so they don't mind being assholes

But these common items in no way answer why these big assholes are in control. Having an education is no big accomplishment and working a long time is hardly significant. We see that these fellows are just the same as anybody else, with little peculiar habits and tastes, with idiosyncrasies and incompetence's like any other corporate member. In fact, if you could take an executive's power and clothing away he would look like and behave like any other "normal person". Well clothing can be bought but what of this power? There are two other items left on the list - getting through the levels and their AQ's. Somehow the acquisition and retention of power must be related to these two items.

We have seen that one's height in the tree seems to be proportional to his AQ, so to be an executive it seems to warrant a correspondingly high AQ. If not, you may not be able to treat people as assholes so as to properly climb upon them; you could get trampled easily if you are going to be "nice". In addition the way in which one climbed through the AQ phases was critical - keeping the AQ and position in equilibrium. By paying attention to these two aspects, somehow power and height was attained. But before we examine more closely this process of getting power, let us look again at corporate environments.

THE CORPORATE PLAYGROUND – OR BATTLEGROUND?

You may have noticed the thick interplay between these boardroom characters. You may also have noticed that details were skimmed over rapidly except where a more general topic was tabled. Notice also that much of the hard-line basis to the questions was bottom line based... the profit motive. More important, you saw a constant jockeying for "one upmanship" positioning as each one worked quite diligently on his AQ levels.

It was easy to see that no one had any reservation when the opportunity came to treat the other members like assholes - no reservations at all! Obviously, if this is really the case, then the best way to be successful is to accept the fact that you will be an asshole and work away at being the best (asshole that is!). But not all people believe that climbing up the ladder is a success measurement, nor do all wish to be an asshole. On the contrary, some people would prefer to keep away from the ladder altogether. Others may want to achieve a certain height and then just do a good satisfying job. But whatever your choice is, it must be realized that the very nature of a corporation generates competition for positions, success, money and power. It therefore becomes difficult to simply sit quietly and not be involved. You cannot sit in isolated oblivion while those above are constantly watching you for better production or mistakes, while those below are after your position.

Whatever the case, power of some sort must be learned and used. Similar to playing a football game, you must first learn the game rules. Power, in the corporate game, is different in that nobody willingly tells you the rules of the game! So while your AQ rises, you are forced to play by learning the rules through trial and error - fairly dangerous to say the least! And if one of the rules is that you must become an asshole, then it is not surprising to see many people fail to play the corporate control game very well. If we look at people in a company, we could group them into four types:

Type 1 Climbers - they want to climb to the top.
Type 2 Plateauers - they want to climb to a level and stay.
Type 3 Cavers - want to be left alone.
Type 4 Grunts - don't give a shit either way.

These four types make up the players on the corporate playground, each with varying levels of skill and knowledge of the POWER GAME rules. For those who do not play well, the playground clearly becomes a battleground for power as those who learn the rules will trample the other poor slobs. Most professional people work to better themselves in a company. This means position and power or status and money, so they are immediate entries to the battleground. With the exception of Type 4 Grunts, these players must learn both offensive and defensive techniques if they are to reach their objectives. So the Climbers must know both defensive and offensive rules well, while the Cavers need to know defensive techniques. The Plateauers need offensive rules to attain the desired level - then they need to know good defensive rules to maintain their status. If you don't believe this then just consider the following statement:

All people in a corporation are there to be nice to each other all the time. They all try to give each other help in getting more money and they all work in harmony to make the company a lot of profit - so they can share it. Seniority is determined solely by the number of years in the company because this is directly related to intelligence and productivity...

Is this absolute unadulterated horseshit or isn't it? Maybe the following is more applicable:

All people in a corporation are trying to take advantage of each other so that the company makes money. The idea is to minimize the help to the other guy so he doesn't get powerful enough to screw you or take away your money. Anyone who shows any sign of weakness is trampled and crippled. At regular intervals groups will get together to hold a trample contest, seniority being the reward for standing at the top of the heap. This way the company has the fittest people at the top...

Is this the way it is or is this just crap as well? How about this scenario:

The people who are at the top of the company are there because they are smarter and superior to the others who work for them. Order is accomplished by a loyalty to the company that in turn ensures productivity. People work to better the company and to ensure that the smarter ones are assured more money. Because the top people are so smart it is normal that they choose the smartest ones from below them as their successors...

More bullshit, right? What about this:

All people in companies are motivated by profit, power, prestige or some combination thereof. These are derived directly by being responsible for the improvement or betterment of the company, as assessed by someone in a more senior position. Order, control and efficiency are accomplished through a hierarchy of power and authority systems that are based upon management techniques. Those who learn the techniques well will be more likely to affect productivity and attain the spotlight needed for assessment. The one's who learn and use these techniques the best are the ones most able to rise to the top...

Is this no closer to the truth?

Although we have cited some fairly wild extremes, the truth probably lies in a combination of the four scenarios. Whatever the case, maybe, the scenario is like a playing field with the attainment or retention of power being the goal. So what are these rules? Let us first examine the playing field.

We have already looked at the executive playfield. It was called the BOARDROOM. This was where we saw the executives use their skills and apply the game rules - to the best of their abilities. And because the executives represent the elite highest order in a company it goes without saying that they should know the rules best. Right? After all these are the people with the most power and they make the most significant decisions. Moreover, they make the most money, and their chosen means - MEETINGS? Why? IDEALISTICALLY meetings provide the following:

- They are the most effective way to accomplish many tasks.
- They are the best way to communicate information to others.
- They provide a necessary face-to-face interaction.
- They provide the means of developing collective solutions.
- They create the feeling of being part of a team.
- They can develop a sense of joint commitment.

This is what meetings are <u>supposed</u> to provide! As the executives tell you. "*Meetings are an intensive way of involving others in solving problems and making decisions which can improve the company or its people. Involving others in problems or decisions is the most effective way to ensure that they will accept and support the results.*" That's the way it should work - and in many cases it does work this way. But we have a strange paradox associated with the business of meetings.

Meetings are everywhere, taking up significant time, effort and money. It is estimated that if you are a middle manager you will spend 35% of your working time in meetings. By the time you are an executive, this percentage will have reached upwards of 50%. That is a significant amount of time! The strange paradox is that even though meetings take up such an incredible amount of time, the technology of insuring that meetings are indeed effective is given little importance.

What this means is that the key rules to be learned in the boardroom meetings are not taught, but learned through experience - possibly by trial and error. And yet these rules, which obviously give one effectiveness and control in meetings must be one of the key ingredients to the attainment of power. The clues to these rules we have seen in the executive meeting. Here we saw the executives joust and jockey for positions of status. And we saw them deal with all those difficult decisions, didn't we?

At any rate, the whole point of the chapter is to identify the idea that corporate meetings and their players constitute a very significant segment of any company. In addition, we can undoubtedly pick up the most pointers on how to play the corporate game by looking at those who play the game the most and those who have scored the most power goals - the executives. They have obviously had the best chance to develop their skills to the highest level wouldn't you think?

In the next chapter we will begin to unravel the secrets of these executives. We will see that there are two **transitions** that climbers must go through so that they can play well on the corporate battleground. We will see how, as one proceeds through these transitions, one successively trades his technology for newer and more effective power tools.

II

A CLOSER LOOK AT EXECUTIVES

THE CORPORATE EXECUTIVE

This chapter is dedicated to the corporate executive - that pillar of strength, power and perseverance. When he has the AQ Virus, he is the great asshole that all those pyramid climbers try so hard to mimic and replace. It is time to look more closely at this super being's secrets to success – at least the way I have seen it work! Understand that I do not want to pick on the executive as I have lived there myself but... it is pretty clear that an executive represents the group that has best succeeded in the other's eyes. He has the most power and makes the most money! If there are special secrets, then these are the ones to scrutinize. In particular, it is time to have a closer look at what gets them there... and what keeps some there.

I know these guys and gals use AQ tactics. And what are those tactics? Well it is all about using tools to keep your AQ in line with your position. It is also about changing positions as quickly as is possible when disequilibrium threatens.

As we look deeply into the successful executive's behavior we will see that most of the time they really are the assholes that they try so hard to be and that they use special tools to help keep the status. Somewhere and somehow the executive acquires special weapons of combat that allow them to survive and prosper in the corporate arena. What they do is develop a special set of verbal and tactical weaponry to keep their position in line with AQ. But here is the strange part: these tolls and tactic are not taught in business and management schools, they evolve though personal experience. And they seem to work! The funny part is that these are universal!

Let me illustrate this process. Let us say that you are a blooming executive and that you have an AQ that is too low. As you spend most of your executive life in meetings, you can use this venue for adjusting your AQ. You can create assholes by using simple statements. Suppose new staff is invited in to make a presentation. When they finish, tell them you don't quite get how it benefits the company and they need to make a better presentation on the key benefits. That creates a few assholes and you get on their list too. But note that there appears to be a more lofty motive in your little attack. It is for the good of the company, not for AQ alignment, right?

Now consider the other situation where your AQ is higher than your position. Guess what needs to be done here? You need to raise your position... or you could end up a victim yourself, ending up on one of those slides down the productivity curve. Well, the same tactic as above would work if your superiors were there. They would think you were a great corporate citizen and maybe promote you.

Suppose you want to get the AQ up really fast and can't be bothered waiting to get a few assholes at a time? Why not send a memo around recommending some cuts in budgets? That's sure to get a bunch.

Finally, suppose you can't change your AQ alignments at all? Well, I have seen many take advantage of this as well. Take this as your AQ signal to move on... leave to a new job. Take a hint and get out while things look good so you can get decent referrals. Impress the seniors, and then get out. Otherwise you could be on the slide down before you know it.

I know this is a simplified example but I have observed hundreds of common tactics like these that executives like to use. As you proceed through this chapter, you will begin to see what some of those tools and tricks are. It may become obvious what you need to do to be like those great executives you may admire - so you can also make a disgraceful climb to glory. Maybe working like a dog is the hard way to climb. Maybe paying attention to your AQ is a lot faster... and easier?

THE EXECUTIVES – WHAT MAKES THEM SO GREAT?

Ah yes, the executives of a company! They can be the ones that everybody looks up to. They are the result of special training and capabilities, representing a special breed of skilled management people who maintain order and progress. Nothing could be further from the truth, especially if we look at Steadfast Meats as a shining example of these superior beings. In previous chapters, we realized that they were just a bunch of normal assholes - just like everybody else. But if we pierce the management veil, we find that they do have some common characteristics and some specialized talents. First, let us pick out some key characteristics from their profiles.

Franklin Hardass started with a degree in engineering, with a tenacious yearning to better mechanical processes. He learned to control people and he concentrated on the improvement of the company. He learned to be strong, unyielding and hard, standing his ground against more senior people. Through courses and experience he learned how to control meetings, subdue emotions, focus energy and develop commitment.

Angus Steadfast attained an engineering degree but was also part of the founding family, so he had a special advantage. He helped coordinate and design plants to become a good engineer. With time against him, and some peculiar quirks, he became a stubborn uncompromising dictator and bullshitter. He also took several additional courses. He became a huge loudmouth has-been.

Scab Dancer started in various trivial capacities but nevertheless created an impressive resume. He also had a formal education. He was able to find ways of bettering financial balance sheets through taxation and depreciation. He learned to dance around unwanted problems and to attack others in the name of the financial well being of the company. He knew how to ask the right questions for the good of the company. He also took some extra courses.

Murk Muddler formally educated in law, impressed one of the executives and was needed to defend employees during bad times. His ability to confuse contracts and legal issues allowed progression. He developed repulsive, gross and offensive habits, which assisted him in being more effective in matters of negotiating and contract destruction.

Flash Spreadsheet with a degree in engineering, had a tendency to fall into jobs by being in the right spot at the right time. He had a tendency to fall into the shit pile and come out smelling like a rose. He had developed the abilities of plagiarizing and being a pain in the ass. By indulging in some special courses, Flash was able to maintain his position.

Herb Hoyle also an engineer, learned from others to quickly become a good corporate citizen. His dedicated problem solving abilities led him to be viewed favorably by superiors as promotional material. Because of his insatiable need to solve problems, he had not developed management skills. He was viewed as a nice guy, probably reflecting the most vulnerable executive of the group.

Slink Wirlwind educated as an economist, impressed top executives with an unlimited supply of deals. He was a fast moving promoter, able to make good presentations and was an aggressive bullshitter. He was always looking for deals that would better both him and the company. He was skilled at avoiding being caught.

Scoot Blastoff an engineer as well, had an uncompromising pace to socialize and develop people. He had extravagant tastes but for the most part got good performance from people. He had become a good negotiator with an insatiable desire to delegate. He was smooth, quick and expensive. He sometimes created excessive confusion.

From this summary, we see that the climb into middle management was aided by some special service, accomplishment or luck in the lower depths of the company, but not one of them seems to be an exceptional hero. What is really relevant here? They seem to have a formal education but do you really think they remember their training? Not on your life! That is what I call **the first level** of training... useless and forgotten except for papers (degrees) on the walls and a bit of has-been bullshit now and again to scare the troops into believing they are smart. I have yet to meet an executive who had a clue about the things he learned to get a degree. Believe me, executives do not maintain their status by being technically competent! This was abandoned years ago.

There is a **second level** to note. If we should look back into the profiles, we see that in addition to being educated formally, certain business courses or degrees (business administration, commerce, finance, economics) were earned. Franklin, for example earned a degree in business administration. Scab, already somewhat trained as an accountant, supplemented his arsenal with commerce. Both Slink and Scooter added business administration to their lists. The backbone of a company… and the backbone of the second level of training is… you guessed it… PROFIT and THE BOTTOM LINE! Not exactly a surprising conclusion, is it? I have yet to meet a successful executive (I said successful) that did not know about profit and the bottom line. In a high level meeting, did you notice that good executives were always focused on finance – the bottom line – as it is commonly referred to (budgets, profits, revenues, etc.), and those things that affect it (efficiency, cost benefits)? This is the new "technology" for the executive.

But now comes a new clue. I call this the **third level** of training. It is even less obvious than the second level. The more prominent executives added some very interesting courses or outside specialties to their credentials. These were a mixture of interesting techniques revealed by the course titles. If you cannot recall the details, here is a short list of examples:

- Exclusive Executive Manipulators
- National Groinkickers
- Boardroom Brawlers of America
- Hedging
- Dress to Kill

- Super Scabbing
- Sidestepping to Fame
- Choosing your Corporate Victim
- Tough Kookie Tactics
- Brotherhood of Loudmouths
- Belligerent Tactics
- Shabby Business Practices
- Direction by Misdirection
- Business Facades
- Narrow Outlooks

Sounds silly doesn't it? But these silly ideas represent "courses" from hard knocks experience that provided certain valuable skills not acquired at school. The reality is that these are really not taught in school at all… guess you knew that all the time! The reality is that these executives did learn some tricks from somewhere. They are picked up as extra "tactics" that were needed to deal with and to move through the **"Time of the great transition"** that I will explain shortly. What is particularly interesting about this process is that I have observed these same tactics in boardrooms around the world, whether it is in government, Fortune 500 companies or even the smallest company. If we look closer, in fact, we would see that the ones who have progressed the fastest (Franklin and Scab) have taken the most "courses"… or perhaps learned the most effective tricks.

There is a time in every executive's life where he is groomed, or grooms himself for the title of executive. The ones who get here and stay here appear to have learned a very effective set of tools that I call weapons… through that third level of training. If you have ever been in a room with some of these experts, they can cut you to ribbons and make a fool out of you or your presentation in an instant. For this reason, I call this weaponry the **Executive Arsenal**. You may wonder why I choose to call these an arsenal. Two reasons: They truly are weapons used to disarm, immobilize or injure and I guess we may as well keep focused on that human posterior again... the arse as it is commonly referred to. When you get through this chapter, you can judge for yourself how appropriate this is.

THE GREAT TRANSITION

At some point in one's corporate life, if one is to climb upwards into the upper echelon, fly with eagles, sit high up in the tree; one must go through the Great Transition - sort of like a corporate menopause. This happens somewhere in the middle management phase when one has to start letting go of that which he has learned and been trained for - to become immersed more in the methods of business and management. Towards the end of this period, he must also develop his arsenal in preparation for the move into the upper management and executive echelon. If he fails, then the process will be difficult and perhaps even disastrous. The Great Transition involves getting your degree in the second and third levels of training.

If I could possibly summarize the Great Transition, it would probably be that period of time where there is an urgent need to understand and adapt to dealing well with "Boardroom Brawling". I say this because executives spend more and more time in meetings... the boardroom... that is where they jockey for position, power and recognition. If you were to spend most of your time in meetings, it would make sense to gather up a new expertise in performing well at meetings. Clearly, some must be weapons that allow one to survive in the boardroom - that place where executives spend the majority of time. Clearly you can't use your technical skills any more so what can you do when AQ Disequilibrium knocks on your door? My contention is that the majority of the Executive Arsenal is therefore made up of weapons used in boardroom brawling so as to adjust that AQ. It turns out that there are actually six arsenals executives use.

These are the secret tools that keep AQ's high. They will be dealt with in detail later. Now we have a new profile of the top executive.

- They usually have forgotten the discipline they used to get the position.
- They have picked some business related education or experience.
- They have developed boardroom brawling techniques.
- They have picked up "bottom line" savvy.
- They have learned to treat people like assholes.
- They are not shy about successfully telling people they are assholes!
- They made it through the Big Transition into management.
- They have somehow successfully come through the Great Transition.
- They have a very high AQ.

Because an executive has moved into a world where boardroom brawling and the use of this arsenal takes up a majority of his time, this distinguishes them from the pyramid below. But they have usually elevated the AQ through the AQ phases of calling, treating and telling so they are good at it. This means that they can treat others like assholes and get away with it as part of normal function. It is this aspect that one must pay attention to. The executive arsenals are just the tools that allow the executive to stay in AQ Equilibrium.

And this little aspect is one of the most significant secrets that executives learn... the art of AQ Equilibrium using the arsenals. How do they do it? Well these tools are very effective in creating assholes so if you need to get the AQ higher to maintain your position, use the tools. If, on the other hand, you find your AQ is too high and you need to elevate your position, try using tools to make yourself look good... at the expense of creating or maintaining assholes. And where is this best accomplished? In the boardroom or in meetings of course!

BOARDROOM BRAWLING

One final word about the most popular AQ training ground... the meeting or the boardroom. It is pretty clear that the executive spends a lot of time in meetings. Estimates vary but this time can be around 60%. That is why the meeting is the true place of performance for an executive. This is the prime battlefield. I can also tell you that there are many executives appearing on this battlefield who do not know how to align their AQ's... and have not learned the arsenals very well. In reality, things don't always happen smoothly in meetings and many are quite a joke, but if there is an executive present who is skilled in AQ Arsenals, he will surely be the one to watch. Some executives are quite aggressive, and in many cases, self-centered individuals with appetites for power and an insatiable appetite for ego food. Others are just plain stupid. It is not uncommon to see some fairly volatile performances occur when there is a possibility of others threatening a position. Remember the big meeting at Steadfast Meats?

It must be remembered that the vast majority of executives did not get to their position in the tree by just sitting there and doing nothing. And it must be also remembered that these people are constantly being threatened by newer executives lower down who are themselves similar in aggression and needs... and with their own arsenals. They had to replace someone or they had to be better than someone else. So these boardroom meeting places are truly places where great performances (funny or sad) take place.

It has been suggested that meetings are a means of accomplishing critical things fast. We listed several main purposes. It has also been stated that executives are decision makers. This means that they must get to the heart of things fast and make effective decisions on spending money, resolving problems and making profit for the company.

Well, if it worked this way all the time, it would indeed be an efficient corporate world. The truth of the matter is, however, that many executives are not well trained and meetings do not work efficiently all the time. As I said before, the reality is that they do not have much of a clue about technology... or the area of expertise in which they may have started. That makes it a new scene for all. What's the substitute "technology"? Why the "bottom line", "cost benefits", "budgets", "efficiency", "revenues", "commitments", right? It is this that forms the basis of meetings and if you don't believe this, then my advice is to keep away from this group. But I have noted another interesting phenomenon at these meetings that makes it easy to apply AQ tools effectively. I call this the Laws of Executive Regression.

THE LAWS OF EXECUTIVE REGRESSION

It is not hard to understand how many executives become outdated and helpless in a family of "eagles" or "condors". Most have forgotten their chosen technology... called a *has-been*. They also require a new area of expertise, called finance... that makes them *dummies*. This means that has-been dummies are running companies. Think back to the big meeting we had at Steadfast Meats. Is it surprising, in view of this and the infection of the AQ Virus to understand why the following laws are in force at an executive meeting?

175

LAW 1	Information deteriorates as it moves upwards in a pyramid.
LAW 2	Meetings bring together a group of incompetent assholes who attempt to exchange and present ever deteriorating information in such a way as to impress each other so they can become bigger assholes and affect company profit.
LAW 3	The more general or simple the topic is, the more likely it is that it will get blown out of proportion.
LAW 4	Authorization is quickly given when the authorizers cannot be held responsible should the project fail and when all of them can claim credit should it succeed.
LAW 5	The greater the cost of putting a plan into operation the less the chance there is of abandoning the plan - even if it becomes irrelevant.
LAW 6	The higher the level of prestige accorded the people behind the plan, the lesser the chance of abandoning it.
LAW 7	Rationality will prevail only when all other possibilities have been exhausted.
LAW 8	The more distant the participants are from the facts the more likely they are to believe what they hear.
LAW 9	The amount of time spent on detailed discussions can be inversely proportional to the financial commitment.
LAW 10	If a majority of the attendees are responsible for a miscalculation no one will be at fault.
LAW 11	Justification procedures will become more difficult as the cost decreases.

Can you better understand why so many meetings are such a joke? These are the laws commonly working against progress and these are the laws that help AQ's rise quickly. It is this mixture of idealistic approaches and regressive obstacles with which we see executives functioning. This is the corporate playground where the rules are learned and executed by has-been dummies. But alas, these executives have these new AQ skills to make up for their incompetence. I call these the Six Executive Arsenals.

THE SIX EXECUTIVE ARSENALS

I call these arsenals because they are truly weapons executives under the influence of the AQ Virus use and they are so consistently applied internationally I would swear executives have a secret rulebook that comes to them in a flash of light when they attain the title! I have classified them into six major groups, many of which were used in the meeting in a previous chapter. The arsenals I have observed are the ways by which you create assholes rapidly so as to re-align your AQ or impress someone in order to change your position. In many cases, these are just tactics that seem to work for people caught in the corporate mire of protecting position, power and profit.

Arsenal 1   is the **Offensive Arsenal** used to attack an opponent.

Arsenal 2   is the **Defensive Arsenal** and covers the weapons needed to create a defense against the offensive weapons.

Arsenal 3   is the **Aversive Arsenal** used as offensive or defensive methods. They are there to round out the arsenal.

Arsenal 4   is the **Trouble Makers Arsenal.** It is designed to deal with people who need to be put in their place

Arsenal 5   is the **Cultural Arsenal** and it includes methods outside the boardroom to also align position

Arsenal 6   is the **Manipulators Arsenal**. It is used to get your way.

Let us now get into some details of what these are and how they are deployed to protect power, ego, and position under the influence of a bad case of the AQ Virus.

When you read these, please understand that I am not attempting to give you advise on how to climb faster or develop new tactics; even though these are exactly what many end up using. What follows is a compilation of what *I have observed* in many "successful" executives. It may even be that you see merit in using these yourself, but before you do, please read the last chapter.

THE OFFENSIVE ARSENAL

I have observed in many corporation that there are a select set of behaviors that I classify as the **Offensive** category. It contains four main types of weapons designed to place an opponent on the defensive. I am sure you have seen these in action many times. Please be aware that although I use "you" as the potential deplorer, this is not meant to insinuate that you should do this.

Let's use an example here. Grizz Buzzard is the VP of Finance.

He is a surly, wretch of a man with a personality like a torn boot and absolutely no sense of humor. He is an old fart, protective of his position but skilled in his arsenals. Flick Smoothy is a new VP, not so skilled with his AQ tools, highly energetic, a fast learner and can shoot from the lip.

THE CONTROL: ALWAYS CONTROL THE FLOCK

Have you ever noticed in meetings how there is someone who is able to keep order and control? Well there are many tricks to doing this. Controlling the flock requires the ability to keep any situation orderly by forcing a direct focus on relevant issues.

Essentially it is like acting as a policeman who maintains order by simply being present and by also being equipped to enforce the laws if necessary.

If we relate this to the boardroom, these laws are not usually clear but the need for order and focus is critical. Otherwise the issues at hand are not likely to be solved. In addition, the

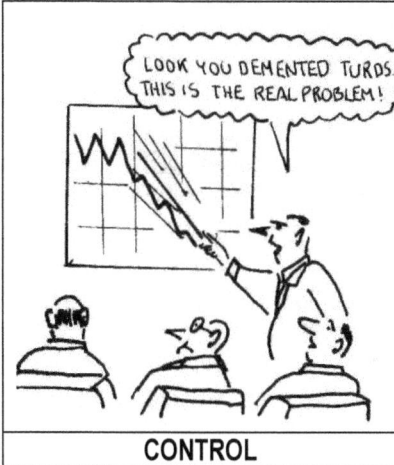

"controller" must be able to coldly attack to enforce order so that a focus is maintained. This is not a place for some babbling pipsqueak. Any meeting can typically become disorderly if volatile discussions take place or no conclusions are reached.

CONTROL

Can you remember how Frank took control in the big executive meeting? Remember him assuming power and saying: *"The meeting will be one hour in length, our objective is..."* Next meeting, pay attention to how the executives do this. It is simply wrapped up in what you say, how you say it and how you reinforce it. That leads to another tactic. Imagine Flick frothing at the mouth in his presentation as several others in the room chat amongst themselves... Can you hear old Grizz say: "*Excuse me gentlemen, but if you cannot repeat the last statements in this presentation, then I would advise you to get out of the room.*" That is control.

THE PROBE: PROBE AND FIND THE STATE OF HEALTH

Probing is a boardroom technique which directs a query at the opponent and puts them on the defensive immediately. The best probes are used by the financial people focusing on basic corporate objectives and needs. This assumes that you, the Prober, are concerned about the company and are taking the responsibility of looking out for the company's interests. And what are the company's interests? Profit, results, efficiency and control are key company interests. By setting yourself up as this shining, concerned company representative, you automatically infer that your opponent has clearly not followed the same interests so he is immediately on the defensive.

Probes are also designed to see how well prepared, how healthy or how organized your opponent is. In addition, Probes are usually left until some material, proposal, project, etc. has been presented or circulated. If you are in a meeting and you want to see how well prepared people are, try a Probe. Suppose Flick Smoothy has just gone through the proposal to spend a bunch of money. Grizz

THE PROBE

asks: *"How much will it save?"* or *"How much will it make?"* or *"What are the benefits?"* and *"Who is responsible?"* If Flick is not prepared for this, he can kiss his proposal goodbye. If he is, good for him and Grizz looks cool for asking. If he is not, Grizz will be licking his beak. You may have fallen victim to these questions yourself and been embarrassed for being unable to justify. It is pretty amazing how such simple questions can dethrone people, get order and add to an AQ list. Now if you get caught yourself, there are tools that help you escape.

THE COUNTER: COUNTER AND FRUSTRATE YOUR VICTIMS

I will bet you have seen this tactic many a time but paid little attention to it. Countering allows one to take advantage of his position in the hierarchy. Counter weapons are especially capable of placing the opponent on the defensive quickly. The insinuation process that it conveys is that those who are in the authoritative state to make decisions are not yet convinced of whatever someone is attempting to convince them of.

THE COUNTER

The Counter is a move that immediately assures that the one who uses it is superior in position to the one it is directed at. It is an easy way to create an asshole. The effect is the same even if it is a group that a Counter is directed at. Counters will also focus upon the material of the meeting whether it is presentation, report, exchange, or whatever. There are many ways of countering or putting people back on the defensive. Imagine that old Grizz has asked you to justify your cost benefit analysis and you have indeed bent over backwards to explain it to the old fart. He then counters with a statement like "*I am not yet convinced of the 12% rate of return*" or "We *cannot support that until you provide backup analysis to your rate of return calculation.*" I have seen people absolutely steaming with rage after some rotten SOB persists with counters. Remember what happened at the big meeting? Well think about reversing this so you are the one doing the Probe and the Counter. Here's another tactic from the offensive arsenal.

THE ATTACK: ATTACK AT THE SIGN OF WEAKNESS

Attacking is conducted in various ways but the purpose is the same - to identify issues, which need better analysis and clarification before decisions can be made and before the company commits to some course of action that it may regret. An Attack is meant to make someone look stupid for not being thorough enough in convincing the members. Although Attacks can be conducted diplomatically, only the positive group of tree dwellers like Eagles, Hawks, Owls, Falcons, etc. have a tendency to do this constructively. The negative group like

THE ATTACK

Vultures, Condors, etc. will use such opportunities to totally disable and sometimes cripple victims quite permanently if possible. These are used to impress others, including your superiors, as it shows you are tough and really concerned about the bottom line. Let us go back to Grizz Buzzard and his Probe/Counter on Flick. Flick has now tried to explain to Grizz what the cost benefits are and is getting a bit emotional. Grizz is in a position to Attack. All he has to say is: "*It is obvious that you are not sufficiently prepared.*" or "*You have been totally misguided on corporate objectives.*"

Note that an Attack is launched when a failure has been perpetrated. This means that a probe and counter have identified the fact that someone has not "done his homework". Again, an Attack can be done constructively. You may attack someone by saying "*Our discussions indicate that we have insufficient material at this time. We should therefore continue the discussion when we have reviewed it.*"

These are attacks, however, that assume a fatal conclusion. In reality there is never any guarantee that your opponent is indeed totally disabled and that he will take the crap that has been handed to him. The Probes already discussed were a form of indirect Attack method. They just attempted to subtly identify weaknesses. There are many ways that executives attack. One is called Hotseating, an aggressive statement that puts someone on the spot. Another popular one is to use Power, reminding someone that they better watch out who they are dealing with. The one that is really effective is the Challenge where you need to put up or shut up... or the Threat that infers you better be right or there are serious consequences.

Ok, you now have some insight into how simple sentences can keep you generating assholes while keeping your position in line with your AQ if you are creating too many assholes. But this is only one side of the coin. How do executives protect themselves from other executives who are good at the Offensive Arsenal? You guessed it. It's called the Defensive Arsenal.

THE DEFENSIVE ARSENAL

The **Defensive** group covers the weapons needed to defend one from the offensive weapons. That's how executives escape some of the tactics when they are probed or attacked. How many times in a meeting have you thought: "*Man, how did he manage to get out of that pickle?*" or "*Boy, I wish I was as fast with my mouth as he is.*"

CONCEALMENT: HIDE THOSE WEAK AREAS WELL

There are various needs for Concealment at certain times, regardless of whether such concealment is done on purpose or because someone is poking around looking for a weakness. If for example, you have conducted what you considered a thorough study, written a great report and made a super presentation, then you would expect that the executives would just honestly accept your recommendations - right? That could well be the case but it is not likely, for the various probes, counters and attacks that are aimed at your material could quite easily reveal a weakness or something you just bloody well forgot at the time. You can rest assured that the detection of this - even if honestly admitted - could easily result in a total destruction and refusal of all your hard work. Why else do you have executives? So do you take the chance or do you

CONCEALMENT

184

launch a play to conceal your underbelly? Most likely you will elect the ploy.

On the other hand, if you know that the executives are only interested in whether the idea makes money, then why would you present all of the triple integration formulas from differential calculus that were used to prove new theories in Wave Form Transmission. Anyway, a consultant did it so why not just reference it with the hope that they will not have some freaky haired mathematician there to make you prove the idea? So why not launch a little ploy to conceal your underbelly? Most likely you will elect to use the ploy. It matters not whether you have purposely tried to conceal or you are trying to cover yourself from some vicious probes - the idea is the same.

There are many ways to do this, but one of my favorites to observe is the Flash. This is where the weak areas where you can get nailed are flashed by so fast no one has time to really catch it. If Flick Smoothy was doing a presentation of his proposal and wanted to make sure that Grizz Buzzard didn't get a chance to grab his calculator, he would flash through the section on the detailed numbers. The other is to provide so much detail it is impossible to digest it in a meeting. The most popular, however, is Veneer. The report, the pictures, the body all looks so professional and filled with good stuff but in reality it is only superficial crap.

THE DIVERSION: DIVERT THEM AWAY AS FAST AS YOU CAN

The Diversion becomes necessary when the enemy is close to finding your cover-up. Experts at this are indeed entertaining. The weapon of Diversion is used to keep your foe away from the potential problem area - so that the problem is not revealed.

Sometimes you yourself may have detected the weakness only when the enemy has sniffed around a bit. If that is true, you must act fast to divert him away from any vulnerable area. If for example, you just realized that there is a simple calculation that is wrong - where some totals don't balance - but you are close to agreement, would you not want to keep old Grizz Buzzard, the VP of Finance away from his calculator? You surely would, especially when you have heard horror stories about the mean bastard demolishing so many proposals that had poor arithmetic.

THE DIVERSION

In fact you may even jump on the table and try to make the old fart laugh so you could distract him - in shear desperation! Remember that a diversion is required to get your enemy away from the area where he happens to be sniffing around, but as yet has not found the smell source. Just like the bird, you need to distract him in a different direction - away from the nest.

To perform a dance on the table may be a bit more than you are willing to do, so you can try the Fast Forward method on old Grizz. This allows you to flash by or skip the sensitive area. Another one used by politicians is the False Battle that creates an irrelevant focus, thus avoiding the real battle. A really cool diversion is Word Clouds that combine a set of meaningless words that make a simple sentence impossible to understand. The simple statement of *"We need some help"* becomes *"The technological interfaced methodology suggests that we need a logistical systemized input for some help."* by throwing in a few clouds. It can be seen how word clouds can be used, not only to confuse issues, but to also quite effectively create diversions.

Another of my favorites is the Piss Off where the guy gets the attacker to become emotional. Once that happens, he is now dethroned. Well, there are many others that executives use. Pay attention to this in the next meeting.

THE DEFLECTION: DEFLECT THEM IF YOU CAN

I love these when they are used expertly. The Deflection is required when your opponent has realized that you may be hiding something and he decides to come in for a closer look. In other words our little birdie has failed to foil the intruder who is heading straight for the nest. Now what can the birdie do except try to deflect the intruder in some way. At this point, deflections can take some fairly dramatic forms depending upon how desperate the bird is - even to the point of using itself as bait. It may even try some direct attacks. This may seem hopeless, but many a tiny birdie has thwarted some rather awesome intruders - right?

THE DEFLECTION

Let us, for example, carry on with old Grizz Buzzard, the VP of Finance, who is pecking away at his calculator, adding up the numbers which you know are wrong. As his beady eyes shine with glee at his findings you know four things. First, the numbers are not relevant to the main conclusions. Second, the rotten shit will discredit the whole report if he finds it. Third, you are close to an agreement, and fourth, you better do something fast! But as you are thinking, Grizz puts his calculator down and speaks with a sardonic grin: "*Mr. Smoothy*" he crackles, "*I hope that the quality of your report is not reflected in these simplistic calculations which I detect in error.*"

Well, what would your answer be? How about this: "*Yes, Mr. Buzzard, I noticed this just this morning but it was too late to change it. Fortunately, this section, which was specially checked by your Assistant Vice President Mr. Wimpledork is not relevant to our conclusions. The rest I have double checked myself.*" What do you suppose Grizz would counter with? In fact, Wimpledork didn't check anything. But he is not there and how would old Grizz know? Grizz is not likely to attack because he may injure himself. This is a successful deflection. Mr. Smoothy just pulled a Bluff with some Bullshit thrown in to a Buck Pass, three other deflection weapons. And even if Grizz finds the truth later, by taking the senile old Wimpledork to task, it would be too late. Anyway, Mr. Smoothy could use some other weapons like Play Dumb or Delegate. These are certainly not my favorites but nevertheless they are used all the time.

One of the most effective... and funniest to watch is called the Sideball. Say someone has just put Flick Smoothy on the hot seat. Flick simply, and slowly turns and looks at you. Now you are on the hotseat and have said nothing. If you don't feel you are, Flick may try a Buckpass by saying: "Well, perhaps it's time for this quiet fellow to have a say about the topic." Or worse, Flick says: "Let's hear from you since you said you were knowledgeable in this area." There are many ways to do this and if you ever pay attention, you will see some real skills in this area.

THE RECOUP: RECOUP TO MINIMIZE LOSSES

So now you have been wounded by another skillful executive. The Recoup is the name given to a group of weapons used to minimize your wounds. It must be assumed that someone has not only ignored your diversions, broken through some deflections and put you on the spot. On the other hand, someone may have just caught you off guard and you are on the spot. Either way you are up shit creek to put it mildly. Like the bird, your enemy has found the nest and your direct attacks are not effective - your wing is broken and you must get away before you get eaten. The Recoup weapons are used when there is little left to do but minimize losses. Remember the old adage of "*he who turns and runs away lives to fight another day?*" The Recoup is the same idea.

THE RECOUP

Let us return to old Grizz Buzzard who found the little errors in addition on Page 353 of Flick Smoothy's proposal. Let us assume that Flick did not have a deflection ready and that Grizz made the whole report look like a joke. In addition he made Flick look like fly shit on a swatter. So what does a demoralized, beaten Mr. Smoothy do? He executes a Recoup: "*You are absolutely correct Mr. Buzzard, the figures are incorrect. I only wish you to understand that I and three of my staff have worked 18 hours a day for the last week in order to prepare the report for*

*the meeting. Two are suffering from fatigue because they were
so dedicated - the stress undoubtedly caused the errors."*

How does Grizz eat that one? As it looks now, both are at a
standoff since they both have made each other look stupid. Flick
did not recover completely, but he did manage to regain some
dignity and a little bit of territory - by executing a Recoup. In this
case he executed two other Recoups, the Pressure and a Sting.
The Pressure tactic means you tell him: "*Do you have any idea
how hard everyone worked to get this out in time?*" Then you
follow with a Sting: "*Why are you being such an asshole about
this when everyone has worked so hard?*" One of my favorites is
the Groupy when the shit hits the fan. This is where you start
naming others who were involved in misdirecting you or helping
you screw up.

THE AVERSIVE ARSENAL

Admittedly, some of the previous stuff got a bit serious. Yet I
have encountered countless examples of these tools. But the
funniest one I left for last. You may read these in total disbelief
but nevertheless there are repulsive creatures in a company who
dare to use certain measures that are in a class of their own.
These special weapons although not popular, are classed as
Aversions. Nevertheless, they are boardroom brawler
techniques and deserve special attention. These aversions are of
three main varieties, all of which affect the sensory organs of the
opponents. If used effectively, they are sure to undermine any
serious opponent or even neutralize any stoical boardroom
atmosphere. These are the art of emitting gaseous materials,
commonly referred to as **Farting**; the art of exhaling gaseous
material, known as **Cigar Smoking**; and the art of expounding
with colloquial injectors, known as **Cursing**. Although there are
many other techniques, these are by far the more important
ones. The use of these, however, can be a very delicate matter

190

so it is recommended that one treat these techniques seriously since if applied poorly they could cause irreparable harm to an executive. Let us recall Murk Muddler, for example. Not only had Murk built up the confidence and stupidity to use these tools, but he had also developed the ability to sometimes use them to his advantage. Here we go… bite your tongue when you read these four techniques.

FART Provides the use of smell to set the mood of a meeting
CURSE Provides a way of dramatizing and emphasizing
PUFF Provides a way of dulling the senses of the meeting attendees
OUT Provides an exit strategy if all else fails

THE FART: GAS AND SMELL TO SET THE SPELL

Since our hypothesis suggests that by the time one reaches the executive level, the majority of people look upon you as an asshole, it may not be out of place to behave like one and fart. In fact, if you have ever sat in on a meeting and listened, sometimes it seems that all these assholes are just farting profusely at each other to get each other's attention and to see who can make the biggest smell. All the groaning, grunting, wheezing and huffing

AVERSION IN ACTION

are just preludes to the vast varieties of sounds and smells which fill the room. The real fact of the matter is that a well-placed, controlled fart can work to one's advantage.

Just imagine the situation where someone is being hot seated. There has been dead silence for 45 seconds. The guy has gone beyond a time period where he can recover. Do you think that a loud resounding Fart would break the tension? How about the situation where three guys are in a small room and after three hours of trying to get a contract signed, the guy wanting the signature just keeps farting quietly? After a mere 20 minutes, a lack of breathing air, watering eyes and a dulled brain, could cause the other guy to sign and leave quickly. And what would happen at a long presentation where someone was just pouring out obvious bullshit and dribble, and no one knew how to stop the guy politely? Do you think a high frequency "Hisser" would break up the meeting? You better believe it!

Now suppose you are in a deadly argument at a meeting - every fraction of a second is crucial to maintaining good counter attacks. If you let out a squeaker after purposely crossing your eyes, and the squeaker slowly rumbled into a brap brap brap, do you not think you would destroy your opponent's advantage? What if you totally ignored the fact of what you had done? All this may seem a bit silly but there really are some silly people in corporations. Just imagine, if you will, being able to time these? Would this not give effectiveness to farting as a brawling tool? Suppose experts in this field began to associate rather unique and effective smells with the ingestion of certain body chemistry catalysts like prunes, beer, pepperoni, eggs, sausage, pizza, exotic fruits and so on. These, in combination with various liquids, could get one a considerable variation in caustic penetrating odors. The control of audio aspects could also be quite a science and depend somewhat on one's posture as well as how one positions the cheeks of his ass. The effects could not only be notable, but varied in purpose. For example:

RESOUNDING (Braaaap) This one would have a tendency to startle people, particularly if loud enough.

LOW FREQUENCY (Burruurruupp) This would be an awesome variety since it carried the suggestion of forthcoming gas of incredible volume.

SQUEEKY (Peeeweeeww) Usually would need to tighten the cheeks for true squeaking. It would usually be non-scary but if coupled with a wicked smell, it could really upset the balance of a group.

HISSER (Sissssississ) Hissers would be excellent for shifting blame. It would be hard to detect where they came from unless they were too long in duration. You could easily make the guy beside you look pretty bad if you blamed him shortly after emmission.

WHISTLER (Pheeeeeep) Whistlers would be fairly harmless but good for breaking tension immediately, the smell being fairly mild. But they would be good warning of what's to come.

WET PLOP (Phhoooploop) Wet ones would be extremely difficult to execute without shitting oneself. This is why they would have very serious effects on opponents. The possibility of forcing the more serious act of shitting one's pants would always have enough awesome connotations to curtail everyone's activities for at least one minute.

ROLLER (Rrbop rop rop rop) Rollers could be sustained for considerable duration. They would be effective by absolutely destroying an opponent's thought processes, particularly if one could continue the Rop Rop without any notice to the activity.

SILENT The silent ones, with smell, would be most effective in destroying the atmosphere of a staunch boardroom, particularly if one could keep the activity going for a while. When the air was watering everyone's eyes and they were breathing loudly for air, you could be sure that their brains are dull. That would be the time you could get agreement on an issue quickly.

On the other side of the coin, one would take care not to fall victim to an expert farter. One would not only develop his own special control, but he would develop immunity to others. Yes, I know that timing and control are not easy to master as farts seem to have their own exit strategy. But I knew a guy who could fart on signal. Another could fart when scared.

THE CURSE: A FEW VULGARITIES AMONG GENERALITIES

Yet another method is the **Colloquial Injection** technique. Once again we have Murk Muddler as an example of an expert. Angus Steadfast also started to gain some expertise in this area. Colloquial Injection simply means that you inject foul four letter words into your normal sentences. But another note of caution - you must use the principle of **Grammatical Polarity**. This idea is based on the fact that at the one end of the grammar spectrum are the well structured, precisely worded and educated literary "flowery" type words which make up a sentence. The other end is made up of unstructured vague imbecilic word conglomerations that are mostly meaningless and gross swear words. As an example of the first type we could say: *"With clear perception, we now understand the set of unprecedented and paradoxical conditions which have led to our disagreement on this issue. Perhaps it is only now that we may undertake a more constructive approach to a clearer cooperative venture."*

At the other end, we have *"Ya fuckers ought to know what ya fucked up - hey - now that youse all gots shit in your goddam pants youse all smellers. Now all youse fuckin cockwalapers gots da fuckin goods to giver shit - hey?"* We have here two attempts at grammatical poles, to say the same thing. Now let us combine

194

them through the Grammatical Polarity and Colloquial Injection: *"With clear perception, we now understand the set of unprecedented and paradoxical fuckups which have led to our disagreement on this issue. Perhaps it is only now that you imbecilic, ignorant cockwalapers may undertake a more constructive approach to a clearer cooperative venture."* The polarity principle simply merges the two extremes for effect.

One may ask what is the effect? First it goes without saying that the better formed the sentence and its content, the more clearly it communicates its purpose and brings connotations of knowledge and education. Secondly, there is nothing like a strong, disgusting colloquial expression to project anger and disgust - unfortunately it may also project ignorance and stupidity. Thirdly, a well-constructed combination creates clear communication with superior knowledge but with a projected intensity of anger or total disgust. In the example above, if such was stated in a corporate boardroom, in the first instance the speaker would be classed as an educated wimp, while in the second case just a dumb klutz. The last one could well be an angry executive asshole. So what do these injections do for the arsenal? Let us list some:

AMPLIFICATION It goes without saying that *"Fuck Off"* is a much stronger emphatic expression than *"Go Away"*.
FEAR There may be some significance to the use of a colloquial to inject fear. This is probably because the use of a colloquial is usually associated with people that have more muscle than brains and are creatures living under physical laws. *"I'm goin to kick your fuckin head to shit pulp"* is an expression which would inject more fear *than "I am going to kick your head "* - it sounds like it has more adrenalin and force behind it.
EFFECT There are certain words which are just better suited to saying things more effectively. You can look through the dictionary quite a while trying to find a word equivalent to "fuckup" in intensity of meaning.

SURPRISE There is the element of surprise, which if dealt properly, always leaves a feeling of one-upmanship. This may be purely psychological but every little bit helps.

Essentially, however, the whole idea behind the Injection Method is to play the "Big Tough Guy", since all big tough guys use swearing as their means of communication. If you are to be tough then you must make sure that you use the expressions wisely, otherwise you could be reduced to a "muscle brain" and defeat your purpose. Consider someone who says one of the following.

"What reasons do you have for being late?"

"What ya late for, ya shit the bed?"

"You are late. What excuses do you have for being so fucking irresponsible?"

Which one has the most energy and effect behind his question?

THE TROUBLEMAKER ARSENAL

Inevitably there are always people that you encounter in a meeting that are truly a pain in the ass... oops, there goes that preoccupation with the human posterior again! I call them Troublemakers. There are those who will really do their very best to piss you off - possibly because of that instinctual white collar urge to help you raise your AQ. Some do this directly by design while others do it without even knowing it. Some are really good at it and some are superb. Others are mere amateurs. This part of the AQ story we devote to dealing with these people - helping them raise their AQ's equally fast.

Troublemakers are a special breed of people at meetings since they are usually breaking meeting rules. Many of these rules are just simply acknowledged as universal unwritten protocol. For example, sleeping, being late, wearing jeans, or clowning around are just not readily accepted habits at executive meetings. For this reason, it is usually quite easy to use sarcasm in making the guy look like a real turkey, also adjusting your AQ. In applying an arsenal tactic, you must keep in mind that there are two different levels from which they are applied - either as a chairperson/presenter or as a meeting member.

I bet, if you really think about it, you have seen some skilled tactics in putting troublemakers in their place. I will bet that you have also thought in hindsight it would have been really cool to have said or done certain things... if you had thought of it. Well, let us learn from the skilled executive again. In dealing with troublemakers at meetings, it is useful to begin with a subtle intervention - sort of a Probe to see if you really want to fix this turkey or to find out if you should let the situation alone. Upon deciding positively, however, it is best to keep in mind that you should try to use one of the Offensive or Defensive tactics. Firstly, you must identify the type of

TROUBLE TACTICS

victim and what the victim is doing wrong. You must then quickly invade his private space by catching him off guard with a strong statement directed at him. Your chosen statement must sarcastically amplify his violation and leave him looking like an asshole.

In my studies, I have classified about 30 different troublemakers. For example, the Whisperer, the Cell Phone Junkie, the Yapper, the Bustler, the Doubter, the Snoozer, the Bragger, the Interrupter, the Gossiper are just a few. And of course, you must remember the Pecker and the Slurper. The names I have given these are a good clue to what these troublemakers do. When you sit and watch a pro at this, it is quite beautiful to see... and sometimes very humorous! Let's look at a few of these.

The Whisperer is always the stupid jerk that is carrying on some secondary conversation while someone is talking. The whisperer and his neighbor make it difficult to concentrate as they giggle, smirk and whisper. Needless to say, even if you are just in the area of these problem people, you can become irritated or distracted. Assuming that you are doing the talking, the best way is to stop talking and stare at the whisperers. The longer they continue, the more likely it is that other attendees will join the stare - to embarrass them. When they realize what is going on - usually 30 seconds is sufficient enough time, after which you can choose your shot.

If you are standing, it is most effective to walk over to the pair and then stare at them. If you are simply a meeting attendee whose patience is being tested, just before you choose your shot time, say to the speaker or chairman: *"Excuse me Mr. Waffle, would you hold on just a minute...?"* Then turn to the guilty pair and give it to them! You can get a double-digit score on your AQ!

The Snoozer is always fun to deal with since it is so easy to literally scare the shit out of him - taking him by complete surprise. His position is so indefensible that the embarrassment you can serve to him is indeed superb and everlasting. If you can do it well you will remain on his AQ list forever. Snoozers are bored, lazy, tired or just stupid to be attempting such things at meetings. Although they offer no direct threat to meeting attendees, it is fairly distracting - and certainly distasteful - to see someone slumped over or snoring quietly in his chair. If the guy is a hard sleeper, you should walk over and shake him - then Hotseat him by asking him to repeat the important message being covered.

Some Snoozers are light sleepers so that he may awake quickly at any movement or silence. He may even be partially aware of what is going on. It is best in such cases to simply switch the focus to him from wherever you are to make sure that everyone's eyes have moved to the appropriate culprit before you Hotseat him.

The Doubter is another painful schmuck who just does not believe anything. His sole purpose, it seems, is to exude negative expressions like: *"There is no way", "I don't believe it", "It won't work", "I'm not convinced".* The biggest problem here is that you are always wrong until you can prove otherwise. If you remember the Offensive Arsenal, this was a Counter technique to find the state of your health. On the other hand, the doubter could just be a stupid asshole. The best way to deal with a doubter is to either reverse the scenario or shut him up through a Reversal. Answer with a question that extracts something from him that you can attack. The simple act of asking *"Why?"* will usually start the ball rolling. If you can extract something from the doubter, you will usually have something to counter on or attack.

Quite often the attacker is seen launching various types of attacks at other members of the meeting. Some attacks may even develop into personal arguments that can get fairly hot and heavy. It should be noted that these attacks, being unlike those discussed in the offensive arsenal section, are more personal in character. The key here is that some personal attack has been launched or an argument has developed. Before such behaviors embroil the meeting participants, it is best to stop the attacker or argument as quickly as possible. It is best to physically and verbally interrupt a fight. Then, unless you feel some compassion, attack them to make them look foolish.

The Bragger is the intolerable asshole that must tell everyone of his accomplishments, credentials and other things, which are supposed to receive immediate respect, admiration and superior status. Thus credentials, professional status, age, length of service, affiliations and old projects are all used to create "superior" input or assessment. The Bragger can be heard saying: *"I've been in the business 20 years so how does this whippersnapper think he knows more?"; "I have a PhD. in Geology so I know the interpretation is horseshit"; "I produced research papers on the topic 15 years ago and I know damn well it won't work"; "Who do you think taught the little squirt all he knows?"*. These little comments are typical of some "has-been" whose power and prestige is lost somewhere in the past. There is nothing more irritating than some senile fart who demands superior technical know-how because he has worked forty times as long as everyone else or because he got a PhD. in 1893.

Braggers are typically obnoxious in their presumed importance and it is a treat to be able to reduce them down to their deserved stature. It is best, therefore, to Hotseat them by forcing them to firstly explain the relevance of the stated background and then secondly making him clarify the details behind the conclusion.

Remember the Slurper? This was the unbearable Suckhole who slurped his way upwards. These people constantly seek out and focus on anyone higher up who they try to impress. They look for approval, credit or whatever from any senior – even if it is at the expense of others. In addition, Slurpers are typically wimpy little shits who couldn't make a decision if they had to. They are particularly painful and obvious at meetings, almost to the point of precipitating physical anger - to strangle the awful insipid creep. Slurpers are best at agreeing with seniors, either to cover their ass or to try to gain approval. They are typically saying, *"Why I agree with what Mr. Supershit said. He was so thorough that I could add little"*. The fact is that the little shit couldn't add anything if his life depended on it. *"I am equally concerned about what Mr. Sidewinder is worried about"* or *"Golly gee, shouldn't we check with Mr. Highness first"* are Slurper tactical expressions.

Contributing virtually nothing except to take up space, these crawly vermin have good instincts towards survival, by plagiarism or taking the same stance of someone who is in power. It is, of course hard to trap him or make him look stupid because he is quick to attach himself to someone else's idea. Your frontal attack is therefore a potential attack on someone else as well. You must therefore take care in not discrediting the one with the original idea - unless of course it is absurd. Remember that Slurpers retain their positions by suckholing, plagiarizing, leaching and applying well-placed liplocks on lofty corporate members. Willy Liplock and Barf Chapstick were good examples of Slurpers.

Finally, there is the Pecker, who we all know about. He was the one, like the Slurper who got to be a humungous asshole using similar tactics to the Slurper but with a new dimension. The Pecker has a good memory with which to peck at someone. Usually, therefore, it is even harder to catch this vermin because he remembers details he can use against you. Peckers are also like leeches, having great accuracy and strength. *"I agree with Mr. Almighty on the issue, why did you disagree with this very issue yesterday, Flick?"* is a typical example of how the Pecker adds new dimensions and why he is a more dangerous cockroach. *"I think Mr. Greatgruffer has brought up a very important aspect of the issue. So why is your staff, Mr. Greaser, violating this?"* or *"Grunt, you said 7 years ago that you would follow this principle. Why are you now going against the President's mandate?"* or *"You, Mr. Blastoff are over budget, not us. I concur with Charlie Costcrotch here that we need more control - because of people like you"*, are other examples of how a Pecker, under the wing of some lofty flyer, uses a Shot to Hotseat you.

Although we now encroach on Boardroom Brawling more than problem people, we must still admit that this type of creep is a problem at a meeting. He so obviously is a scab who attempts to start trouble and to make others look bad. Such unconstructive stuff is therefore a real problem - and difficult to deal with because he is perhaps adding some information (albeit conflictive) to the meeting. What needs stopping, however, is the potential emotional turmoil or subjective fight that can result.

So we have here a form of Attacker, which we have already dealt with - but some extra tenacity must be added to the recipe. Now there is the possibility that what the Pecker is doing is Hotseating someone you would like to get anyway. If that is the case, you should amplify the situation to get the response - then attack the Pecker. You may be able to get two birds.

THE CULTURAL ARSENAL

Just for a bit of a change of pace, we need to target a few tactics outside of the boardroom. I call this the **Cultural Arsenal** and includes some very useful tactics indeed. I call these the Five C's of Corporate Culture. Remember that not all executives climbed up on the backs of boardroom attendees. Here is a list of the Five C's:

Credentials: it's what you take that makes you great
Communication: speech and pen for forceful men
Class: shiny and clean with look supreme

Compatibility: smiles and flirts even when it hurts
Cultivation: groom the branches to increase chances

You probably get the picture already and can identify several in the company that have gotten their positions through "other" means. Let us pick one that I call Cultivation. Cultivation refers to the process of aiding your growth up the corporate tree by providing bits of fertilizer in special places - better known as horseshit. Oops, there's that posterior thing again! Effectively, you cultivate your superiors with bits of horseshit to help your growth. Very simply, it is difficult for anyone to give you a promotion if they do not know who you are, what you have done and how you fit in.

WHY DORK AND I BOTH FLASH IN THE PARK. HE'S AN EXCELLENT MAN FOR THE VICE PRESIDENCY!

CULTIVATION

So the best way to seek paths and promotion is to let people know - influential people that is - who you are. Consider the example of finding a new job as a Mining Engineer out of the country. Where do you start? If you had maintained a friendly correspondence with 3 or 4 guys who had themselves moved to international locations, then you would know exactly where to start and your odds for success would be much higher than if you fired off four resumes to international companies. Whether there is a genuine friendship or not is insignificant, the fact of the matter is that you have used fertilizer (correspondence) to cultivate your growth (new position) up the tree.

So cultivation refers to a personal process usually conducted away from the office - otherwise it does not get personal. And it may work in reverse as well. Consider the Chief Engineer working at a mine in South Africa - he is looking for or knows someone who needs a good engineer. Now, since he just had a letter from you - an old buddy - guess whom he recommends as a good engineer? You may in fact be an incompetent slob but you are deemed ok simply because he knows you.

Well the same idea works in a company. If you go to the club and slurp scotch with the executives, these fellows will know you the same way and when something comes up, your name is right there as a candidate without even applying. In the meantime the silent competent fellow who goes home doesn't have a chance in hell.

Cultivation is like the business of sprinkling manure all over the place. This way you could get some nice growth occurring. For those who have a natural tendency to socialize, the task is easy. For those not so inclined, socializing with those on your AQ list may not be so easy. In any case, procedures involve getting personal with those who may somehow assist your growth and this requires after-hours frolicking. Clubs, socializing, partying and just general entertaining are means whereby the horseshit can be spread around. Playing golf with the VP's, going to wine tasting parties with the Chairman, drinking cocktails at the Exclusive Arseholes Club of America, or having the VP's over for a good piss up, are all good cultivation scenarios. Here you can bullshit them to death on how good you are - or they are - and how great the company is, embedding you in their minds as a good candidate for joining their ranks.

Many a promotion has been acquired this way, by simply placing yourself in the conscious part of someone's brain. Here you can be "pulled out" whenever a position occurs - as first choice. Some slurpers make their way to great heights this way. *"It's who you know and how you blow"*, they will tell you with a straight face, and mean every word of it.

A good example of this principle in action is our friend Willy Liplock the Assistant Vice President of Operations. Willy started by going to University just like anybody else. He was a personable enough guy, but with a gusto for bullshit. Willy was a bit different in that he knew how to cheat on exams and plagiarize with the best of scabs. So many of Willy's school friends just considered him a cheating blowhard with few engineering abilities. But Willy was developing something that would become particularly useful when he finally went to work for a corporation. He was developing abilities in the Cultural Arsenal. Willy cheated his way through Engineering and spent a lot of time at the Faculty Club "mingling" with University professors. He also joined B.F.O.A (Bullshitters Federation of America) where he received honorary recognition within two years. This is how Willy got his first job - at a bullshitting free-for-all at a BFOA Convention - where he met some fellow bullshitters who were looking for new engineers.

It didn't take Willy long to join local golf and squash clubs as well as the Amiable Asshole Association (Triple A it was called), knowing where the managers hung out. Here Willy would bullshit and play with his boss and other managers, telling them how great he was. It was here that Willy met Scooter Blastoff from Steadfast Meats. It didn't take long for Scooter to offer Willy a job at one of the plants as an engineer. Willy went on to play with top people at the plant, moving in as Chief Engineer because the plant manager liked Willy.

He, Scooter and Willy got pissed out of shape and had great fun every time Scooter came up for a visit. When an opportunity came up for a plant manager position it was almost automatic that Scooter choose Willy. *"He's a goddam good engineer"*, Scoot would say, *"He's going to go a long way in this company"*. The truth was that Scooter and Willy got caught in an old whorehouse near one of the plants and Willy quite faithfully never told anyone so it was not difficult to understand why Willy was such a "good engineer".

As Plant Manager, Willy now had new games to play and new players to rub shoulders with - not surprising to see him move to head office as Assistant Vice President. Willy, in just five short years moved up the ladder very quickly - getting into positions where his ability as an Engineer meant nothing - his credentials, his cultural attitude, and his bullshitting ability were more important.   But remember that if you have the audacity (courage?) to bullshit someone, you are actually treating them like assholes and raising your AQ. In the mean-time, all the poor drips who were technical marvels at school with Willy were still struggling away at junior to intermediate engineering levels because they were working hard and not busy bullshitting.

Ok, one more of the Five C's, Compatibility. If we think back a bit and consider Angus Steadfast, we will recall that he was not chosen as President, even though he was a member of the family. Angus was not "compatible" because he had a funny habit of leaving his fly at half-mast to tease the girls. This little habit was not "boardroom etiquette" and certainly not executive behavior. Murk Muddler was an even grosser example of some odd incompatibilities. Murk may have thought that his vulgarities and farting made him tough and great but there weren't too many other people who thought so - especially the executives. Who wanted to associate with this big fat bilge rat?

Compatibility covers four main areas, mainly manners, etiquette, diplomacy and dedication. Manners and etiquette are needed in meeting wives of executives, other friends, clients, professional associates and so on at parties, functions meetings, dinners etc. etc. If this is hard to believe then think about Murk Muddler being invited to speak at a special wine and cheese party for executive wives. Do you think anyone, even Angus the old piss tank, would want to be held responsible for setting up such an occasion? Not on your life - Murk is not compatible enough with the corporate culture.

Diplomacy is another requirement of the Cultural Arsenal, which is not always mentioned. If you lack it, however, it will surely be mentioned: *"Flash, why did you tell the people from IBM that their proposal was horseshit? And why did you make them so uncomfortable by not introducing them? Is this the way you think we executives behave?"* What about this: *"Suffering hemorrhoids, Angus, where the hell do you get the gall to tell my wife that her ass is wider than a jeep? We invited you to the party in good faith and fun"*. Diplomacy is the skill of handling affairs without causing hostility. If one does not have it then it is surely quite noticeable.

Dedication is another form of compatibility that requires mention. Dedication means loyalty to the company and its people. It is important that an executive shows his dedication strongly and visibly. Thus, dedication becomes more of a compatibility with the company and company affairs. For example, you cannot have a Vice President walking around a shareholders meeting, with his brain pickled on martinis and his fly half open, saying: *"Those figures are absolute turkey turds, the Vice President of Finance doesn't know how to count the number of peckers in his crotch."* Instead, he should be walking around in a well-pressed suit, spiffy and trim, smiling coolly and saying *"We, of course, feel that those figures are quite conservative. As our Vice*

President of Finance points out, the next quarter's earnings will show our company in the true light of excellence. He is especially competent in his area". Dedication requires that you and the company are one, and that you are compatible with it - even if it hurts to admit it.

Compatibility also means that all time is company time - you are available 25 hours a day, without question. You rise to the call of the company with a smile and your briefcase. Somewhere along the cultural climb, your attitude must change from giving the company your time to taking some time from the company.

THE MANIPULATOR ARSENAL

There is yet another important aspect of the Great Transition that an AQ mindful executive needs to pay attention to. I call this one the **Manipulator Arsenal**. So far we have looked at offensive, defensive and aversive tools to your AQ. We then looked at the importance of dealing with troublemakers and the importance of paying attention to the corporate culture. What we have missed, however, are those special tools needed to create the insidious little ploys and deceptions required to get your way - to fool your opponents, so to speak. To suck people in properly, a ploy is needed whereby a chronological set of planned steps is executed so as to lead someone towards an inevitable conclusion - the one that is sought. If we should look back at the Defensive Arsenal, we would see that there are methods like the Fast Forward and Flash that are methodical ploys to hide vulnerability. Clearly these methods were designed to control the material being presented so as to avoid entrapment and potentially bad issues.

In my career I have identified about 16 key manipulator tactics that make a great arsenal. There are many and you have probably seen them in action or fallen victim to them yourself. It goes without saying that a Manipulator must have a certain cold mentality, without any fear of being an asshole... by treating people like assholes. In general, a good manipulator will show the following characteristics:

- He is well prepared and knowledgeable on his topic.
- He is not easily ruffled.
- He does not make snap decisions.
- He has a clear course of action, concessions and ploys.
- He uses language and grammar wisely - without confusion.
- He has a strong instinct in detecting weakness.
- He is a diplomatic asshole.

So the mentality of being a cool, narrow-minded asshole is a very important aspect of being a good manipulator - and a good executive! It really helps align your AQ.

Manipulator methods attempt to force a required decision or conclusion. This is a particularly useful segment of the arsenal should you be negotiating, selling something or just seeking approval on some proposal. As an executive, it is not likely that negotiating situations can be avoided. Whether it is a new deal, a contract negotiation, convincing superiors, or just a plain con job, the need for Manipulator methods will be inevitable. As the executive moves through the Great Transition, these methods must be learned, used and tucked away in the Arsenal. Let me give you a list of manipulators that I love to watch when they are performing at their best.

Exhaustion: "*Want to go through it again, and again, and again?*"
Tyrant: "*Do you want the mean VP back or do you want to deal with easy me?*"
Lesser Evil: "*Would you prefer to lose a little or take a big chance and lose a lot?*"

Humble Pie: "*I too have been such a twit but I have learned, haven't you?*"

Paper Piles: "*Seen enough material to give up now and agree with me?*"

Lead-in: "*I know I shouldn't ask you why you screwed up but...*"

Deadline: "*We must leave in 5 minutes and a decision must be made.*"

Have you got the idea yet? These are simply ways of getting your way indirectly.

Here is a simple example that I call Exhaustion. Exhaustion depends upon the perseverance of the manipulator. Clearly the principle used is to exhaust the opponents into submission. You can insist upon going through your pitch over and over until they are sick of hearing it. You can hold a sequence of meetings. By the sixth meeting on the same issue, they may be quite happy to agree to your proposal - anything to avoid another performance!

EXHAUSTION

Have you ever sat in a meeting and wished it would end? What about those meetings that are still going strong and it is 8PM, you know your spouse is pissed off and you were supposed to do something on the way home? Well, the pressure is actually on you, not the guy trying to get a deal signed, or get approval for something. Did you ever think this was a ploy to exhaust everyone into submission just to end the horror?

SO HOW'S YOUR AQ TODAY?

Now we come to the end of the executive secrets. The previous chapters have attempted to reveal key ingredients that executives seem to develop in order to maintain AQ Equilibrium. Obviously the ones that do this the best are closer to the top. These we revealed as the essential tools of the executive "trade", making it possible for the executive to truly be the asshole he aspires to be.

We looked at the executive meeting. Here we saw the executives in action, using their tools as best they could. Although the meeting seemed funny and even absurd, it contained many of the brawling and tactical techniques also discussed - they just may not have been obvious.

Before we finish, however, it would be useful to review that big meeting - in terms of what we have just learned. So take a break and go back and read the meeting again. Or perhaps read it in a few weeks after you have sat in a meeting of your own to see how many arsenal tactics you can count. When you finally read it again, see how many of the AQ tools you can identify as you read.

After looking at the executive meeting again, it may have become a little clearer just how the executive operates to deal with the Laws of Executive Regression. The AQ tools are a direct substitute for any technical details executives lack. More important, these tools are typically used to maintain AQ Equilibrium. Some were understandable. Others were disgusting, focused at clearly making some else look like a complete asshole, reducing him to an imbecile. But what is very clear is that the majority are used to protect egos, position, power, money, and the corporate "purpose" of profit and efficiency.

We touched on the six arsenals, mainly the Offensive, Defensive, Aversive, Troublemaker, Manipulator and Cultural. These were just a quick summary but covered in much more detail in Book 2 (*Corporations Stripped Naked 2: Controlling the AQ Virus*) which delves in Management Arsenals as well. We also learned that these AQ tools were developed through the Great Transition. We have looked at all sides in the use of the Arsenals - to illustrate more clearly how to deal with them as well as how to use them.

But here is the crux of the matter. Whether you are aware of it or not, the tools seem to be used to maintain equilibrium and climb rapidly to power because you become an unscrupulous, heartless asshole - if that is your wish. The AQ measurement is your thermometer to measure your progress. The AQ allows you to measure your relationship to others in the company. But the AQ level is directly related to your position. Behind the scenes is this insidious AQ process that creeps into every corporation. It effectively works against you from the first day on the job. It is now time to recap the AQ Laws:

1st BASIC LAW OF AQ'ISM: There exists a natural tendency within any one corporation for any one individual to classify another as an Asshole.

2nd LAW OF AQ'ISM: The percent of Assholes within any company, as viewed

by any one individual at any point in time is defined as one's Asshole Quotient or "AQ" level.

3rd LAW OF AQ'ISM: Any new entry into a corporation will tend to have an individual AQ near zero.

4th LAW OF AQ'ISM: Any individual AQ, given sufficient time, will tend towards 100.

5th LAW OF AQ'ISM: Individual AQ's have a tendency to rise according to a natural growth.

6th LAW OF AQ'ISM: From the date of entry into a corporation, an individual carefully sets out to prove that he or she is an Asshole.

7th LAW OF AQ'ISM: Sooner or later any individual will freely offer evidence to prove that he or she is an Asshole.

8th LAW OF AQ'ISM: AQ's have a tendency to be reciprocal in motion.

9th LAW OF AQ'ISM: Your local AQ will rise to its level maximum within a period of 2 years.

10th LAW OF AQ'ISM: Your level of responsibility must rise in direct relationship to your AQ level.

Do these make a bit more sense now? Accepting these laws as an underlying process is not such a bad thing. You can get a chuckle and you can work it to your advantage b avoiding the virus. Remember the Peter Principle? It reflects the fact that you become further and further removed from what you knew best… you become incompetent! Sorry but that's reality. The AQ tools appear to be the means of defeating this and avoiding those devastating productivity slides downward in position and stature.

Here is the bottom line. If these laws are working against you and your AQ is in Dis-equilibrium, you have three key choices:

1. Raise your AQ to be in line with your position.
2. Raise your position to be in line with your AQ.
3. Leave and zero out your AQ.
4.

Arsenals are used to make this happen as quickly as possible, and the executive, who spends so much time in meetings, has become expert in developing a new expertise. You can learn from them and laugh about it too once you see this AQ process clearly.

There is, however, one other important aspect about the executive that we have neglected to discuss. This relates to the fact that he has come through the earlier phases of the AQ Progression - through middle management. It is in his travels through middle management that he has picked up other tricks and tools that were needed for AQ Equilibrium - the ones picked up through the Big Transition. These tools helped him move through middle management. Obviously these are known as the Manager's Arsenal. Ah, yes… this is another book!

So ends our satire on corporate life. Hopefully you have gained a new perspective on corporations and those pillars of strength at the top. Yes, they were all stripped naked for a while to give you a new look at them. Yes, this was presented as a satire, but in reality I have presented many people and situations that may be more real than we care to admit. In reading all this, you may have wondered what was real and what was fiction. But from now on, at the end of each working day, after all those dealings with your co-workers, just think about a simple question: "**How's your AQ today?**"

12

THE BOTTOM LINE
A ZERO AQ

THE FOUR CHOICES

Here is the bottom line. If these laws are working against you and your AQ is in Dis-equilibrium, (AQ higher or lower than your position) you appear to have three key choices:

1. **Raise your AQ to be in line with your position.**
2. **Raise your position to be in line with your AQ.**
3. **Leave and zero out your AQ.**

Arsenals are used to make this happen as quickly as possible, and the executive, who spends so much time in meetings, has become expert in developing a new expertise, much of the time being ruthless and heartless.

You can learn from them and laugh about it once you see this AQ process clearly. This is your 4th choice. It is however, the most difficult.

4. Don't engage in the AQ'ISM addiction

But be aware! A zero AQ is possible!

If you have ever grown a business, the most glorious part is in the beginning, when your passion is high, you are eager to learn the business, and the people you work with are like family working and prospering together... together, loving every moment of their engagements and efforts, acting as one unit of heart. When you first come into a corporation, your AQ is zero!

Of course this changes as the AQ Virus takes hold and the need to protect ego, position and profits become different when the corporation grows. We have created the executive as the pillar of leadership that has come through the earlier phases of the AQ Progression - through middle management. It is in his travels through middle management that he has picked up these somewhat ruthless tricks and tools that were needed for AQ Equilibrium - the ones picked up through the Big Transition. These tools helped him move through middle management to the position of Executive and it seems that that original philosophy in choice 4 is quickly left behind to create the AQ Arsenals for survival.

So now you have come to see this as a satire on corporate life. Hopefully you have gained a new perspective on corporations and those pillars of strength at the top. Yes, they were all stripped naked for a while to give you a new look at them. Yes, this was presented as a satire, but in reality I have presented many people and situations that may be more real than we care to admit. In reading all this, you may have wondered what was

217

real and what was fiction. But from now on, at the end of each working day, after all those dealings with your co-workers, just think about a simple question: **"What's your AQ today?"**

THE DEEP LESSON HERE?

When you read about all these Corporites and their AQ's, the Arsenals, peculiar habits, striving for power and position, you begin to wonder why it has to be so. And you think about yourself, and how you may be affected (an infected) as well. Why do we tend towards seeing and being assholes? Why do we choose to engage in these darker corporate ethics to protect and climb towards the perception of "success"? In a company full of these people, it seems the contagious aspect of being an asshole increases substantially. I would challenge you to say you have not seen many of these people and that you have not been affected, and infected in some way.

For me, the greatest lesson came when I began to understand that the vast majority of CEO's, Founders, VP's, Managers, and the likes that were deemed to be "successful", especially the ones that were the experts in the brutal AQ tools, also at some point fell from grace, lost their fortune, company went bankrupt, etc., etc.. So many lived through a boom-bust cycle of rise and fall, profit and loss, happy and unhappy. In retrospect, I cannot recall anyone in my business life that did not go through this cyclic process; just as I did myself. Eventually, I had to get out completely because this "cause and effect" process culminates in ill mental and physical health which take the brunt of this emotional roller-coaster ride on this corporate gopher wheel of life.

My lesson was that I got what I dished out. I received what I perceived. I chose these ways and I received what I gave out. What I had not figured out was how come? I never made the correlation of Cause and Effect and the Law of Attraction because it was never clear or obvious that something like this was happening.

Of the AQ Laws, it is the 8th Law that I should have paid most attention to. It states:

8th LAW OF AQ'ISM: AQ's have a tendency to be reciprocal in motion.

In other words, you get what you project. *"Ask and it shall be given"* or *"That which you sow you shall reap"*. It is not hard to understand that is you do something aversive or bad to someone, that there will be some reciprocal actions. The only problem is that you don't always know you are "asking". And you don't know when or how the "given" will be "reaped".

In the AQ process, we learned that the way you think, infer, call, tell, and treat other people has a direct correlation on the corporate position and the way in which you carry out your duties to maintain order, focus and company mission. There is a choice as to how this is done; nice or not nice, good or bad. You can tell people they are assholes and better get with the program or get fired, or you can feel the need to help them get with the program to improve. How you engage in the thought, emotion and deed is always a choice.

In the AQ process, we learned that we have a tendency to put people on our AQ lists because we feel they are assholes. That feeling is again, a choice which arises from a fear, hurt ego, a loss, threat, and so on. Whichever way you look at it, that feeling is determined by one's choice of perception and thus also the potential engagement of emotion. It is that process of thinking that leads to the infer, call, tell, and treat action that you engage in. Regardless, that is a choice that you alone make.

Can you live in corporate life, or climb into executive positions maintaining a zero AQ? Of course you can. It happens when you start a new job, regardless of position. It happens early in corporate life when the CEO and others are one big happy family. It happens when you are passionate about the work and simply accept others, and forgive them for their idiosyncrasies.

So why is it so difficult to maintain this posture to become immune to the AQ Virus? The lesson is be aware and beware!

THE LAW OF CAUSE AND EFFECT

My big lesson was that what has been portrayed as corporate life in this book, does not have to be that way. And I did not have to choose to use these tactics. Why? Because it was my choices that created the Cause energies that returned to me the Effects. But so many times, I did not even know I was doing it. And fear of loss creates a lucrative energy ground of panic and helplessness for doing stupid things.

Regardless of what choices we make we are engaging in a natural Law of Cause & Effect which states that absolutely everything happens for a reason. All actions have consequences and produce specific results, as do all inactions. The choices we make are causes, whether they are conscious or unconscious, and will produce corresponding outcomes or effects. Here is a big lesson; **even the choice of thinking has an effect!**

The Law works the same for everyone at all times. Distilled down to the simplest possible terms, this Law states that for every outcome or effect in one's life, there is a specific cause; poor diet and exercise habits result in poor health, constant and uncontrolled spending results in debt and money worries, not putting effort into your key relationships results in poor relationships and all of the associated issues. Remember that this law is not the same as the Law of Attraction, this is about what you put out (cause) will have a result (effect).

The trick is to know which one you are using at any one point in time, and when you do to use it properly.

The law can also be applied in the physical sense through examination of Sir Isaac Newton's third Law of Motion, which states that "*for every action, there is an equal and opposite reaction.*" If, for example, you were to hold your hand over a candle's flame (the cause) the effect would be that your hand would burn and it would hurt! While this is an extreme example, it serves to illustrate the point very well.

At the point of making this idea of putting your hand over the flame, you made a decision to act on it (cause). You made a choice and then got the result or (effect). The decision you make becomes the cause and the effect is the result of the decision. The same holds true with your personal relationships. If you treat the important people in your life with respect, love, compassion, dignity and honesty (cause), you will experience loving, solid relationships – which lead to happiness, fulfillment and peace of mind (effect). If you use the AQ Tools (cause) on others, what would you expect the effect to be? Kindness? Gratitude? Respect?

The Law of Cause and Effect is the foundation of Buddhism made up of three essential guidelines:

Good deeds bring good results.
Bad deeds bring bad results.
Your own deeds bring your own results.

Every effect has a cause and a condition. A cause and a condition combine to make an effect. All effects have a cause. All effects have a condition. There are no exceptions.

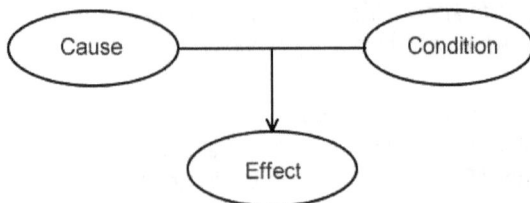

The condition is like planting seed of corn. The corn (effect) will not grow wheat and it will not thrive or grow in a desert. Those are the conditions or nurturing ground for the effect. In the corporate world, the condition is the corporate growing ground.

Think about how this works in the your physical world. Try pissing someone off with your words. Try hugging someone who is pissed off at you. What you give out comes about. So give your brain (and ego) some leeway here and let go of the idea that it does not work the same way with the other energies you create constantly, like thoughts, images, and emotions as well as words..

What is the bottom line? **Be careful what you _think about_ because it may just _bring about_ more of the same!**

What is the other part of your bottom line? **Use the Law of Cause and Effect, and the Law of Attraction towards creating what you want in a positive way, NOT focusing on what you do not want in a negative way**

Have a great corporate life

Ed Rychkun

Be sure to get my sequel book

Corporations Stripped Naked 2: Controlling the AQ Virus

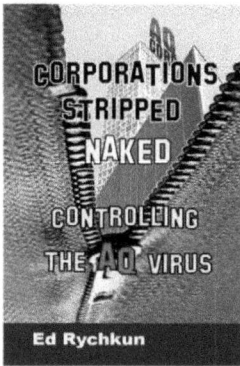

In this sequel to *Corporations Stripped Naked 1: Exposing the AQ Virus*, Author and former business executive Ed Rychkun takes you deeper into the naked corporations secret tactical AQ arsenals. He strips companies naked of their professionalism and glamour to bare the Executive and Management tools of power and control that gravitate into a darker side of the AQ virus and a universal phenomenon he dubs the AQ. Using his own 30 years of climbing ladder to the top, he exposes how top management falls victim to a viral cross between the Peter Principle and the IQ. Using large Fortune 500 companies, as well as smaller enterprises as his stage, Ed relates his first hand experience in maintaining positions of Managers, VP, CEO, Founder, Director, and Chairman. Find out what really takes place behind closed boardroom doors. Get a new perspective on a naked corporation as Ed reveals what the real experts, the Executives and the Managers, use as universal tactics and tricks called the AQ Arsenals to hide their incompetence and climb the corporate ladders fast; and to maintain order and control. See how you can monitor your progress and avoid the AQ Virus of moving to the dark side of corporate life. Get fresh look on how to avoid and control this virus by utilizing to your advantage the Laws of Cause & Effect, and the Law of Attraction.

www.ingramcontent.com/pod-product-compliance
Lightning Source LLC
Chambersburg PA
CBHW070513200326
41519CB00013B/2797